Understanding the Management of Local Government:

its special purposes, conditions and tasks

by

John Stewart

General Editors: Michael Clarke and John Stewart

Longman

in association with the Local Government Training Board

Longman Group UK Limited
Longman House, Burnt Mill, Harlow, Essex CM20 2JE

First published 1988

British Library Cataloguing in Publication Data
Stewart, John
    Understanding the management of local
    government. — (Longman local government
    training board series. Managing local
    government).
    1. Great Britain. Local government.
    Management
    I. Title   II. Clarke, Michael
    352.041

    ISBN 0-582-02552-4

Typeset by Tradeset Ltd, Welwyn Garden City, Herts
Printed by Bell and Bain Ltd., Glasgow

Contents

Other titles in the series

Human Resource Management in Local Government
by *Alan Fowler*

Marketing in Local Government
by *Kieron Walsh*

Organising for Local Government: a local political responsibility
by *John Barratt and John Downs*

Understanding the Management of Local Government: its special purposes, conditions and tasks
by *John Stewart*

Editors' Foreword

This book is one of the first in a new management series launched by the *Local Government Training Board* to be published by *Longman Group UK Ltd*. The series is designed to help those concerned with management in local government to meet the challenges of the next few years. It is based on the belief that in no period has it been so important for local authorities to have effective management.

The impact of government legislation is clear. Each local authority has to review its management, if it is to achieve an effective response. But the challenge is much deeper. In a changing society, new problems and issues demand from local authorities a capacity to respond in new ways. Local authorities have to become closer to their public as customer and citizen; resources have to be managed to achieve value in service; the requirement on all authorities is to achieve effective management of the changes which are taking place.

Effective management requires effective management development. The series is designed to aid the management development of present and future officers — and councillors. It is designed to be *used* by the reader in a variety of situations. While we hope that the books will be used on local government management courses we hope that they will have a much wider use.

They can be used by individuals or groups of managers or as the basis of seminars within authorities. However, the series will truly be a success if it becomes regarded as resource material for use in the business of management itself. We hope that the ideas discussed and the experience pooled will be a stimulus to more effective management.

The series is based on two principles. The first is the need for even greater emphasis on developing effective management in local government and the constant search for improvement. The second is that effective management must take account of the nature of local government. Need for effective management has already been stressed: the case for a separate series particular to local government is based on our second principle.

There are plenty of management books. What we have set out to produce is a series geared to the particular needs of local government. We would want to argue that those concerned with management in local government should draw on as wide a range of general experience as possible. Furthermore we would also want to argue that proper account is taken of the special purposes, conditions and tasks of local government. These books will help the manager to do just that. In publishing them we are not pretending that there is *one right way* to manage a local authority. Rather, we are exposing ideas and questions to help fashion the most helpful and effective approach to the local situation.

The first books in the sequence serve both to introduce the series and to highlight some of the key issues facing management in local authorities. The series will be extended by covering other issues of contemporary concern which require to be tackled if management — and the health of the local authority — is to be improved.

Michael Clarke, Director, Local Government Training Board
Professor John Stewart, Institute of Local Government Studies

Preface

This book is based on a series of papers prepared by the author for the Local Government Training Board as part of a project studying management issues in local government. Four of the chapters (5, 6, 7 and 8) are based on the following papers written by the author with Michael Clarke, Director of the Board:

Public Service Orientation: Developing the Approach (Local Government Training Board 1986).

Public Service Orientation and the Citizen (Local Government Training Board 1987).

The Public Service Orientation: Issues and Dilemmas to be faced (Local Government Training Board 1986).

The Role of the Chief Executive: Implications for Training and Development (Local Government Training Board and Society of Local Authority Chief Executives 1987).

The full list of papers appears in the bibliography.

I am grateful to the Local Government Training Board for funding this work. I am grateful to Michael Clarke for his help, advice and encouragement. Many staff of the Local Government Training Board have helped with this project. Academic colleagues at the Institute of Local Government Studies and elsewhere have made helpful comments on the papers on which it is based. I would particularly thank George Jones (London School of Economics), Rod Rhodes (University of Essex) and Steve Leach, Stewart Ranson, Chris Skelcher, Kieron Walsh and Ken Young (Institute of Local Government Studies). I am very grateful to Kathy Bonehill not only for typing many drafts of papers, and arranging material, but also for organising the many visits on which the paper is based.

John Stewart

Using the book as a work-book

This book is an exploration of the special nature of management in local government. It is intended to assist those who want to develop management approaches for the special circumstances of local government. Although it can be read by all interested in such development, it is intended to be used as a work-book. In the book points are sharpened to provoke thought, issues are repeated to reinforce, propositions are put forward to be built on, questions are posed to seek answers.

Those using the book as a work-book should use the propositions and questions as check lists. They should work through the propositions determining the extent to which they agree with them. They should attempt to answer the questions. These propositions and questions can be used by individuals or as a basis for group discussion. Each chapter ends with a short note on how the material can be used.

Some will want to work through each chapter. Others will wish to select particular chapters. Whichever is done the aim is that those using the book will appreciate that management in local authorities has to be grounded in the purposes, conditions and tasks of local government and will have developed their ideas on management to meet those needs.

I Introduction

1 Understanding management in local government

Key points

▲ *Management in local authorities must be grounded in the purposes, conditions and tasks of local government.*

▲ *The uncritical application of the private sector management model in local authorities will not guide management but will mislead it.*

▲ *Management in local government must support value choice and political processes, for they are at the heart of local government.*

▲ *Local authorities touch the area they govern at many points and management can help realise the potential of local government.*

▲ *Public accountability is a necessary condition to be fulfilled, not a constraint to be overcome. So it is with the other purposes and conditions of local government.*

▲ *The aim must be on understanding of the nature of local government that can inform the management process.*

Management in the public domain

Management in local government has its own purposes, conditions and tasks. Management thinking has no universal principles that can be applied to each and every situation. There are no standard packages. Rather management approaches have to reflect organisational purposes and conditions. If management structure processes and style do not reflect the purposes and conditions of the tasks to be carried out, then management is ineffective.

Management in local government is part of management in the public domain. There are dangers if consciously or unconsciously management in the public domain adopts uncritically models drawn from organisations outside that domain. That is not to say that management in this context cannot learn from management in the private sector, or indeed that the private sector cannot learn from the public domain. Specific management approaches are transferable. What is not transferable is the model of management — its purposes, conditions and tasks.

Yet the private sector model dominates thinking. It leads to the task of management in the public domain being defined negatively rather than positively. It is common to use such phrases as 'management in not-for-profit organisations' or 'management in non-market organisations' to describe not merely management in the public domain, but also in voluntary organisations. The role of management is defined negatively not positively. What the organisation is not is stated, but not what it is. One is told that the public sector organisation does not aim for profit, but not what it does aim at. That is no basis on which to develop a purposive approach to management in the public domain.

The impact of the private sector model goes much deeper. The private sector model defines the nature of management. There are aspects of the manager's role in the public domain which find no ready parallel in the private sector. Those aspects are therefore at best seen as peripheral or incidental features of the manager's task or at worst defined as constraints. One example is the relationship between management and the political process. The phrase 'the costs of democracy' is used, as though it is a special difficulty to be overcome, rather than a basic condition expressing the purposes of the public domain. One does not speak of 'the costs of profit-making' when describing management in the private sector. Such an approach leads either to ignoring the political process or treating it as a problem for management.

It is not merely that the private sector model neglects key elements in the nature of management in the public domain. Uncritical application of the private sector model to the public domain can mislead. Although an approach developed for the private sector can have relevance to the public domain, the approach may have to be transformed in its application.

Thus the marketing role is critical to the private sector model. There is scope for marketing approaches in the public domain and not merely where there are direct trading relationships. Equally it can be argued that for a public organisation, it can be helpful to think of those who use its services as customers. Thought about marketing and customers can be a stimulus to management in the public domain, but if used uncritically it can also distort, unless balanced by a perspective set in that domain. A public sector organisation can and should have many relationships with its public, which are only imperfectly caught by the word customer. Marketing in the public domain can and should be concerned with customers, but it should also be concerned with citizens. It will be about matching provision to need, which is not necessarily the same as demand. Marketing in the public domain cannot be modelled on the private sector alone.

The public domain is constituted not to replicate behaviour in the private sector nor to reproduce market conditions, but to build different behaviour. If the public domain were constituted to operate as the private sector there would be no rationale for the public domain. To make the assertion that the public domain is constituted to operate in different ways, subject to different modes, guided by different criteria from the private sector, is not to argue about the appropriate scale of the public domain. It is to argue that whatever its scale, the public domain has its own purposes, conditions and tasks.

Management in local government

Management in local government has to be understood as part of the public domain, but also with its own special purposes and conditions. These purposes and conditions reflect the nature of local authorities as political institutions constituted for local choice in government and as organisations for the delivery of public services.

Values at the heart of management

Many of the most important decisions that the local authority has to make involve value choices. At the heart of local government is 'the multi-valued choice' (Vickers, 1972). The local authority is not a single-purpose organisation but a multi-purpose organisation, carrying out many different functions such as the care of the elderly, housing, education and transportation. The multi-valued choice is the choice between the many purposes of the organisation, and is at the heart of the budgetary process. The multi-valued choice is choice not about how to achieve, but about what to value.

The multi-valued choice can lie not merely between services, but within services. For in the services of local government values conflict. Conservation and development confront each other in planning: the care of the elderly faces choices between the differing needs of the elderly and indeed of their families; there is inevitable debate about the purposes of education. Value choice is at the heart of management in local government.

Values are present in the choices faced by management in the private sector. Management is not merely concerned with the single value of profit, or even the values of survival and growth. Service for the customers, obligations to staff, and even environmental considerations can figure in the balance sheet of choice. Yet those concerns can be seen as instrumental to concern for survival, growth or profit. Value choice is not at the heart of management as in local government. Local authorities are constituted to make value choice by their elected base. Management must not merely accept that rationale, but must encompass it. Value choice cannot be predetermined and it should not be the role of management approaches to do so.

Elections and the political process

The local authority draws its legitimacy from the fact of election. The elected base is the prime organisational characteristic, distinguishing the local authority from all other organisations in our society apart from Parliament itself. The elected base should not be treated as an incidental feature of local government, but as an essential component of the organisation, legitimating the value choice.

The elected base provides the method of recruitment to the governing body of the local authority — the council. That council can be changed in its composition suddenly by the process of election. The election gives expression to a political process, normally dominated by political parties. It is through political parties that the electorate gives expression to value choice. Beyond the politics of party are the wider politics of the community expressed in demands, pressure and protest.

The management processes of local government are set in a political management system. The key processes of decision making are political processes in which the dominant factors will be the political priorities of the majority party on the council or the balance between the political parties in a hung authority. The management processes of local authorities should, therefore, support that political process and fulfil the requirements of political control. They should be based on the reality and on the legitimacy of the politics of community which are a condition of local government.

Close to the locality in local government

A local authority is defined by the area it covers. From that area it draws its name and its identity. It is the local authority for that area, whether that area is the wider area of a county or the smaller area of a district.

In that area, and normally only in that area, it discharges its functions. The area will be the same for all its functions and for that area the local authority may well have a concern that goes beyond the particular functions it discharges. The local authority can see itself as the local government of its area, concerned with the state of the local economy and with social problems generally. The area of a local authority may have a character and a culture that has its own influence upon the working of the local authority.

Management must be grounded in the areal identification which is local government. A local authority is deeply influenced by and deeply influences its area and those who live within it, and not merely through its functions. A local authority (or at least the two tiers of local government together) is usually the biggest employer and the biggest property owner in its area. It touches the life of its area at many points. It can focus attention in initiative and response. The local authority is close to the area it governs. Councillors and officers may well have a direct knowledge of circumstances surrounding decisions. Even officers working in the town hall are close to the area governed when measured by the scale of agencies of government operating at the national level, despite the fact that they may not necessarily be close enough when measured by the needs and demands of neighbourhood and communities. This local identification is not an accidental feature of local government. It is its very expression, which management should express and support.

The multi-contact organisation

The local authority touches the external environment at a multitude of points. Many travel the streets on behalf of the authority. Many visit homes and buildings. The environmental health officer, the social worker or the policeman are all part of that network of contacts. Much of the work of a local authority does not take place in the enclosed space of the organisation, but in the community. The production process takes place away from the organisation. The organisation that is the local authority cannot isolate and cannot control its production process in the way that a factory can.

The local authority shares this feature with many service organisations but the special feature of local government is the variety of its contacts. A local authority is a multi-contact organisation impacting on the same public at many points. These points include schools, libraries and residential homes as well as the many contacts in the field. The production process is at the contact point. The local authority has to consider itself as an organisation that should not be regarded formally or informally as an enclosed organisation. It is a multi-contact organisation, linked to locality.

Management thinking must understand the character of a local authority as a multi-contact organisation focused on an area. It cannot assume that models drawn from other organisations will always fit the circumstances of local authorities. The challenge for management is to stimulate the full use of the myriad of contacts and to confront the special problems of an organisation whose wide range of work takes place in a multitude of contacts in the locality.

The norms of public accountability

Local authorities have substantial powers which have a deep effect upon the life and welfare of those who live within their area. The use of those powers can raise or lower the value of property. The use of those powers can effect the life-chances of many within its area. The local authority is a tax-raising authority imposing substantial burdens on ratepayers to provide services for the community. The local authority exercises the public power of government. For the exercise of public power, accountability is required.

That accountability is enforced first and foremost by the electoral process. That process gives legitimacy to the exercise of public power, but also holds to account those who exercise that power. Yet public accountability requires more than holding to account. It requires the giving of accounts. Public accountability requires prescribed procedures and scrutiny. In the case of local authorities these are enforced with greater rigour than in the case of central government — perhaps because the procedures are prescribed by central government. A local authority has to publish annual reports and accounts and is subject to external audit. In this respect the requirement of public accountability matches the requirements of commercial accountability. There are procedures governing the awards of contracts. There are formal rights of appeal against particular decisions. The public and press have rights of access to information and to meetings. The actions of a local authority are subject to scrutiny by the ombudsman investigating complaints of maladministration leading to injustice.

Public accountability sets norms for the behaviour of the local authority and for those who work within it. A local authority has to account for its actions to an extent unknown to the private sector. That is right and proper, for the exercise of public power has to be justified. The need to account can, however, encourage caution and the pursuit of uniformity rather than experiment. It can encourage conformity rather than innovation. It is easier to justify stability than change.

Public accountability need not and should not be passive. It can involve more than the observance of proper procedures. Public accountability should be grounded in citizenship. An active citizenship is the guarantee of accountability.

A duty to provide

Laid upon a local authority are a series of statutory duties as well as discretionary powers. The nature of those statutory duties can both be exaggerated and under-estimated. Many of the statutory duties are general in their requirements. The statutes abound in such general statements as 'duty to secure efficient education to meet the needs of the population' or 'to make provision for fire-fighting purposes'. In local government itself, contrary to common belief, there are usually few minimum standards written into the acts governing local authorities.

While the specific nature of the statutory obligations can be exaggerated, the cumulative impact is important in the working of the authority. For although it is possible to argue about the exact scale of those obligations, the weight of those obligations cannot be ignored.

The necessity of maintaining a given range of activities is a condition of management in local government. An industrial or commercial organisation is, also, likely to maintain existing activities, at least as long as the market permits. It is not, however, under a statutory obligation to do so. A local authority *has* to maintain its activities.

The domination of statutory obligation sets a premium on the maintenance of existing activities. That does not mean that management should not search for innovation; it must, for local authorities face a changing environment. It does mean that such innovation must be carried out, while maintaining statutory obligations. The necessities of statutory obligation can be seen as carrying with them the danger of limiting the capacity for innovation needed for community government. That is the danger that threatens the effectiveness of management. It is the challenge to be met.

Need as the criterion

The local authority seeks more than economy, efficiency and effectiveness in the provision of services. There is a fourth E and that is equity. Need, not the market, can be the management criterion for the allocation of services.

The local authority provides services to meet need — and that implies political judgment or value choice, for need is a relative concept. Need has to be understood in the perceptions of those for whom services are provided, but demand cannot replace need. The local authority raises much of its revenue from taxation. Limited resources have to be matched to unmet need and growing demand.

The management of rationing is critical in the management of local government. Rationing can take place in the budgetary process. Rationing can take place in a committee determining the criteria for access to service. Rationing can take place in the field as a member of staff faces demand and need. The criterion of performance must be set by need and need should be a value judgment, grounded in understanding.

Conclusion

The argument is simple. Management in local authorities must be grounded in an understanding of the special purposes, conditions and tasks of local government. Those purposes, conditions and tasks reflect the roles of local authorities as political institutions constituted for government and as organisations for public service. The remaining chapters of this book will be an exploration of that theme, building understanding of what the purposes, conditions and tasks of local government mean for management in local authorities. That understanding of the nature of local government does not encompass the whole of management in local authorities, for local authorities share many characteristics with other organisations. The challenge is not to limit management analysis to that understanding, but to ensure that analysis is always informed by that understanding.

Part II discusses the political process and its implications for management. Chapter 3 focuses on the politics of the council while Chapter 4 focuses on the politics of protest.

Part III examines the roles of local authorities in government and in public service. Chapter 4 considers how the role of local authorities as local government can be given expression through the management of influence. Chapter 5 discusses how local authorities can build service for the public. Chapter 6 focuses on how a local authority can sustain accountability in the citizenship of local government. Chapter 7 discusses the dilemmas to be reconciled by local authorities constituted for the collective of government and the responsiveness of public service.

Part IV contains three applications of the argument to specific issues. Chapter 8 examines the role of the chief executive. Chapter 9 analyses an example of departmental management. Chapter 10 explores how policy discussions can be developed. Those applications are presented to show the implications of the special purposes, conditions and tasks of local government for management. Analysis is not restricted to those implications, but is informed by them.

Those who read and use the chapters will be able to test out how far present approaches to management are grounded in local government and how they might be changed and developed. The aim is that management in local government should support its purposes, meet its conditions and achieve its tasks. How that can be done can only be worked out in each local authority. For it is part of purpose, condition and task that local government is local.

The book is designed to provide an understanding of the special nature of management in local government. Understanding is not sought for its own sake but to assist management for effective local government. Understanding in application is the aim.

Using this chapter

This chapter highlights the need for understanding of the special nature of management in local government. Those using the chapter can reinforce its understanding by the following exercises:

1   Consider the following propositions:

▽   Value choice is at the heart of management in local government.
▽   Management in local government is not merely concerned with economy, efficiency and effectiveness; it must also be concerned with equity.
▽   The political process is not a constraint on management, it sets the purposes for management.
▽   Pressure and protest are a necessary condition of management in local government.
▽   Management in local government has to be grounded in the possibility of innovation as well as in the statutory necessity of service provision.
▽   Local government is local and requires management close to the public.
▽   Management should recognise that the public are customers and that they are also citizens.
▽   Public accountability is the requirement of all management action in the public domain.
▽   The performance of management in local government is found in the life of its area, touched at many points.
▽   Management in local authorities should be management for effective local government and for effective public services, and both are required.

Do you agree with these propositions?
What are your immediate thoughts on their implications for management in local government?

2   Consider the following statement:
Management in local government is the same as management in the private sector
What are the main arguments for and against that statement?

Now consider the following statement:

Management in local government is totally different from management in the private sector

What are the main arguments for and against that statement?

Now formulate your own statement.

II A political institution

2 The politics of local government and the lessons for management

Key points

▲ *As society changes so does the politics of local government.*
▲ *Management attitudes and practice formulated in the past can mislead in the present.*
▲ *Management in a political institution requires political sensitivity and awareness and an understanding of political purpose.*
▲ *The requirement that management in local government should express the legitimate political purpose should mould both management processes and management behaviour.*
▲ *It should also condition management development.*

A changing politics

Management in local government is set within a political-management system and the role of management must be to support the legitimate political processes of the authority. That requires understanding and acceptance of those processes.

There is no common pattern of politics in local government. Politics expresses in its variation the government of difference which is local government. Political attitudes and approaches vary more sharply from authority to authority than processional attitudes. The politics of Conservative Kent, of Socialist Islington, of the Independents of Gwynedd, and of hung Cheshire are all part of the politics of local government. Politics can vary between parties, but also within parties. Politics can change quickly within an authority. The electoral process can bring about sudden and sweeping changes often unanticipated and little understood by officers within the authority.

$\boxed{\text{A}}$* Authorities change from:

▽ a politics of independents (often a politics of geography) to a politics of party;
▽ control by one party to control by another;
▽ a safe Conservative or Labour controlled authority to a hung authority;
▽ an authority firmly and clearly controlled by the majority party leader to an authority in which the political group asserts its power over the leader;

---

*This and succeeding letters identify an exercise referred to in the section 'using this chapter' at the end of each chapter.

▽   an authority accustomed to politics of consensus to a politics of conflict;
▽   an authority where the Social and Liberal Democrats have little influence to
    an authority in which they form an administration;
▽   an authority which is officer-led to an authority in which councillors assert
    their control;
▽   the politics of moderation to a radical politics, whether of left, right or centre.

And some of those changes can as suddenly be reversed. But in all this bewildering pattern, broad trends can be found:

▽   the trend to party politics;
▽   the trend to an assertive politics.

Reorganisation itself in 1974 brought on or speeded up some of these changes. The removal of aldermen, the merging of town and country in the new authorities, and the introduction of payment of councillors through attendance allowances all led to an intensification of party politics — especially in the rural areas where there had been a relaxed political process or a politics of independents. But over and above reorganisation, economic pressures, societal change, the ending of the certainty of expenditure growth and growing disillusion with previously accepted professional solutions led to a new assertive style in local politics. Local politicians became more determined to assert political control and to pursue distinctive policies. With greater political assertiveness came greater political differentiation. The pressures on the polity and the economy of local government have moulded the working of local government through a changing politics.

Broad trends can however conceal the details of change. In that detail, in all its variety, certain common elements can be identified.

(a)   *The growth of party control*
After reorganisation the number of local elections fought on party lines increased, the number of unopposed returns declined, and party discipline on councils tightened. In the urban areas, party politics was already well established so this change was most marked in the more rural counties and districts.

(b)   *Growing differences between the parties over policy*
Up to 1974, the number of issues which seriously divided the main parties in local authorities was limited — sale of council houses and possibly comprehensive education. All parties were committed to significant growth in government expenditure. In recent years the differences between the parties have grown and have been wide ranging in impact. There have been major differences on expenditure policy, on contracting out, on decentralisation, on subsidies for transport and other services and on many other issues. The results of local elections have come to matter in policy terms, and it is perhaps not surprising that the conventional wisdom that local elections are entirely determined by national trends seems today to be out of date.

(c)   *The emergence of the full-time councillor*
The number of full-time councillors has grown. The full-time councillor has been assisted by attendance allowances and more recently by the special responsibility allowance in those councils that have adopted it. Yet that is not the only factor. The full-time councillor is a product of the more assertive style, associated with

councillors determined to secure control over the working of the organisation in order to achieve their policy aims.

(d)   *The growing importance of the manifesto*
The manifesto has grown in importance in some authorities. In those authorities much time is spent in its preparation within the party and it goes beyond abstraction to particular and often detailed, if not always resource-realistic, commitments.

(e)   *The changing styles of leadership*
In some authorities clear political leadership has been established or given greater authority. The leader of the authority has become a publicly acknowledged position and he or she plays the central part in the work of the authority. Dominance in these authorities lies with the leaders and those close to them.

In other authorities, particularly in urban areas which have experienced such leadership in the past, that style is under challenge. The leaders cannot assume that their decisions will be automatically accepted by the group. A new style of leadership is required that does not impose but seeks to find the balance of views. While there are still powerful leaders there is a tendency in all parties for more decisions to be taken by the group in reality as well as in form.

(f)   *The growing influence of the local political party*
It is not merely the group that has been gaining influence, but in some authorities the local political party has gained influence over the group. This tendency is most marked in, if not necessarily confined to, the Labour Party. There has been non-reselection of councillors in both main parties, but the issue of party control over group policy has been raised more sharply in the Labour Party.

(g)   *Challenge to established patterns of working*
The more assertive style has effected not merely policy issues, but patterns of working. The full-time councillor is involved in management issues. In large authorities it is now much more common for leading chairs to have offices in departments. There is a demand for managerial information and for contact with and access to officers at lower levels. The greater involvement in management reflects the emergence on the political agenda of issues about the working of the authority: decentralisation; value for money; contracting out; responsiveness in service delivery. Politics focuses not only on policy, but on the way it is carried out.

(h)   *The hung authority*
In many authorities a three party politics has replaced a simple politics of Conservative and Labour. An increasing number of local authorities in which majority party control had become established and accepted by the officers as giving a certainty of direction and an assurance in decision-making, have become hung authorities in which no party has a clear majority and in which decisions may now depend on committee and council votes. New conventions, new attitudes and new procedures are required. The hung authorities require a new pattern of working which has been found where councillors and officers have been ready to implement it.

(i)   *Political appointments*
In some authorities, there have been appointments of political aides and advisers to support leaders and chairs in their role. In a few authorities it has been suggested that certain senior appointments have been made on political grounds.

There is a clear distinction between the two types of appointment. The first is a political appointment to support a political role. The latter is a political appointment to an officer role.

(j)   A wide-ranging politics
The concern of the councillor may no longer be focused on the traditional services of local authorities. The councillors may emphasise their wide-ranging concern and councils may have to debate the declaration of nuclear-free zones or attitudes to hunting. More widely acceptable, they may express a concern for the local economy that goes beyond their formal duties, for health that goes beyond their specified responsibilities or for issues such as low pay or poverty, which express their role as local government.

(k)   New settings for the councillor
There is a growing political dissatisfaction with the service committee as the main focus of councillor attention. Panels and working groups to explore policy issues have proliferated in some authorities. Review groups to carry out efficiency investigations have been set up in others.

(l)   Communication across the officer-councillor divide
As party politics have intensified, the chief executive and chief officer have had to recognise that the key point of decision-making lies within the political groups. New means of communication have to be found between the officer structure and the political structure. Officer attendance at group meetings is becoming more widely accepted. Elsewhere the link is more commonly built at the leadership level, with for example a meeting of those holding chairs, attended by officers.

(m)   A change of style
There has been a change in style in many authorities. As examples of conflicting tendencies one can consider an authority of the radical left in which decisions-making has been spread more widely. It can be an authority of diffuse decision-making in which many panels and working groups meet and in which councillors challenge the existing 'bureaucratic hierarchies', involving fieldworkers and lower tier officers. The boundaries between council, party group, local party, community groups and trade unions become difficult to draw. One can contrast an authority of the radical right in which the emphasis is on the directing role of the councillor. Chairs see themselves as the managers of the department, controlling chief officers and emphasising greater efficiency and the need for a reduction in local government expenditure.

A complexity of change

The trends and changes set out in (a) to (m) above are not meant to be a comprehensive analysis. They are changes that can be identified in a reasonable number of authorities. Many authorities will recognise at least some of the changes. To others most will seem new and unfamiliar. After all there were still 14% of local authorities remaining independent dominated in 1986 (Widdicombe, 1986). In all authorities there is the need for a capacity to recognise and be sensitive to the nature of change, for change can come unexpectedly and change that is unprepared for or not understood can create problems for those who work within the authority. Management attitudes and practice formulated in the past can mislead in the present.

The implications for management

The changing politics places new requirements on management in local government.

Attitude to the political process

Unless management accepts the legitimacy of the political process, frustration will build up. The senior local government officer has normally been trained first and foremost as a professional. That training does not necessarily equip for work in a political institution. The norms of professionalism may emphasise a uniformity of approach that runs contrary to the requirements of local politics.

Officers long accustomed to a particular pattern of politics may be reluctant to come to terms with change. It is difficult to accept change from a relatively passive politics to a new assertive politics. The full-time chair is seen as interfering in the proper working of an authority. The change from the concentration on chair or leader to the looser decision-making of panels and community involvement is seen as anarchic, and as undermining the formal processes. New patterns of behaviour have to be worked out and that is never easy. Often this is the more difficult because the officers do not readily accept the legitimacy of the changed political process. Yet proper ways of working can only be established if the attitudes of officers encourage a positive approach to political change.

Political sensitivity and awareness

Senior local government officers and increasingly local government officers at lower levels ignore politics at their peril. Unless they are sensitive to the nature of politics in the authority and to how these politics have changed and are changing, they are likely to find much of their work frustrated and frustrating. If they are insensitive to politics, they are likely to draft reports or put issues before councillors in ways that ensure hostility. After all even single words can cause antagonism and not always the obvious words such as 'privatisation' or 'public enterprise'.

Sensitivity is not enough. A senior officer requires political awareness and an understanding of political processes. Time was and still is in some local authorities, when chief officers paid no attention — and needed to pay no attention — to the manifestos of the political parties, knew nothing of the workings of the political groups and were uninterested in the processes of the political party beyond the council.

Increasingly, chief officers and others recognise the need for greater awareness. There is often a remarkable ignorance of and myths about those parts of the political process that are relatively closed to officers. There is a tendency to exaggerate the influence of national party headquarters on local political groups.

The argument put forward here is not for political commitment. That is very different from political awareness. Political neutrality can be combined with political awareness. Indeed it could be argued that political sensitivity and awareness is required, if political neutrality in an officer is not to become political commitment unaware. It is necessary to recognise a political stance in what may be assumed to be a purely professional view.

New skills in communication

Councillors and officers meet in committees and in other settings. Councillors and officers meet and talk, yet they do not necessarily communicate across the councillor-officer divide.

There are skills in communication that can be learnt. There are skills in report writing, in presentation at committees and in group work. But there are special requirements for communication in a political-management setting. If communication is to cross the divide, there must be understanding amongst officers of the appreciative system of councillors, by which is meant the set of beliefs and assumptions through which the councillor interprets communication. There must be understanding of the working world of councillors, the pressures to which they are subject and to which they respond.

Too often, to give but one example, reports for committees are written without an understanding of how they will be read or scanned by councillors working under extreme constraints of time and energy. Reports written for scanning could underline key words in each paragraph and contain a concise opening summary. The most difficult task for the professional officer is to know what is not understood by the councillor. Many seek to avoid jargon, but the most difficult jargon to avoid is that engrained in the officer's very thinking. Experienced officers may not recognise when they use jargon (e.g. calling an engineer a surveyor). Councillors quickly come to learn the obvious jargon, but not necessarily the assumptions that underlie the hidden jargon of common words in specialist use.

Communication is two way. Communication demands from an officer the ability to listen to what is said. Officers can too easily label councillors as 'only interested in their patch' or as 'a political welfare worker'. It is assumed that such a councillor is not interested in policy issues. Once the labelling has been made, words are classified into predetermined boxes. Whatever the councillor says he or she is assumed to be raising a constituency case.

The relationship between councillor and officer is not necessarily an easy one. Over time a chair and a chief officer find, sometimes to their own surprise, a language of communication. But it can often only be achieved with difficulty. Apart from that key relationship, there may be messages across the councillor-officer divide, but little communication. Officers and councillors meet but do not talk.

New patterns of behaviour

In the past, the committee was the setting in which councillors played their role. In that role the councillor received the support of agenda, reports and advice. The authority gave little recognition to any other role. The settings have changed. Over and above committees there may be councillor panels exploring issues away from the formal constraints of a committee agenda. There can be officer-councillor working groups. In some authorities the leader sits in on the management team or there are joint meetings between the management team and the leadership of the majority party. In a hung authority the party leaders may meet regularly with the chief executive and party spokespersons with chief officers.

Chief executives have to build close relationships with the political leadership and, after change, to rebuild. The pattern of relationship between the full-time councillor as service chair and chief officer and department differs from past patterns based on an occasional visit by the chair. Chief officers may have to change suddenly from the simplicities of majority party control to the complexities of the hung situation.

Officers may be called upon to attend the political group and to speak to it. They may go to the political groups of several parties and show both restraint and awareness in the different settings. They may have to respond to manifestos or group decisions. Their task will involve translation between political priorities and managerial and professional practices.

The officer needs the ability to work in new settings and to develop new working relationships, while still maintaining different patterns of behaviour in other settings, such as the formal committee meeting.

New conventions

There is a problem not merely of establishing new patterns of working, but of establishing the conventions that should govern those patterns. For the changing politics has challenged the conventions that have governed the relations between officers and councillors. There are sensitive and difficult issues to be faced.

While this paper has argued that there is a need for acceptance of the legitimacy of the political process in general, that does not resolve all potential issues. In the majority-controlled council, those issues reflect the tension between the right of the majority to govern (widely conceded by all councillors) and the responsibility of the officers to the council as a whole, with all that means for information and advice. Difficult issues have occurred in local authorities on:

▽ the role of the chair in the preparation of agendas;
▽ the right and duty of a chief officer to give views to a committee, even where those views are contrary to those of the majority party;
▽ the right and duty of a chief officer to present information to a committee, even where that information can embarrass the majority party;
▽ the access of opposition parties and individual councillors to the officers and their rights to briefing;
▽ the role of political advisers.

These and difficult related issues are being dealt with in some local authorities, either explicitly or implicitly. New conventions are — sometimes painfully — being worked out, but only where the issues are faced.

In the hung authority a new situation arises. Practices built up for the majority-controlled council are no longer appropriate. New practices have to be developed and new conventions established as they have been, formally or informally, in many of those authorities.

The working out of conventions is not easily achieved. It requires a readiness by both councillors and officers to face up to the issues involved. What is required is a capacity to understand the role of conventions and to consider their implications in changed situation. For management it is a step forward to recognise the role of conventions and the possibility of change in changed circumstances. The aim must be to see principles beyond the detail of practice.

An advance in management

B

If management is to support and respond to the political process, new management approaches are required. At times, it is as if the main procedures of the authority have been developed in their own right, without regard to the political nature of local government. Thus, the budgetary processes of a local authority do not necessarily make it easy to establish political priorities, nor do the information systems in the authority make it easy to monitor their achievement.

Management in a political setting should consider how reports can expose who gains and who loses or whether budgetary presentations can show how the authority's resources are distributed between different geographical areas or client groups and how they reflect the council's priorities.

The manifesto has become an important document in some authorities. But the procedures for translating that manifesto into managerial action have been but imperfectly developed. Some authorities have had the manifesto formally adopted by the council, but that can have little meaning in reality, unless once adopted, procedures are established to resolve the management issues presented. The manifesto has to be related to the financial position of the council. Choices may have to be made between conflicting priorities. Decisions about whether to give priority 'to the problems of the urban deprived' or 'to the needs of industry' have to be translated into council policy and management action. They may involve fundamental challenge to existing activities. Management must assist councillors to face those choices and challenges and to review progress. Manifesto action analysis and manifesto achievement review are required.

Too often management techniques appear to be designed to predetermine political choice rather than to promote it. Cost-benefit analysis that hides value choice in technical calculation can pre-empt a decision rather than assist it. Management techniques for local government cannot be allowed to dispense with the political process. That is not to deny a role to management techniques, but to emphasise techniques that support the political process. The challenge is to build management approaches to do just that.

The development of such approaches requires a new capacity in management analysis, in which understanding of the inter-relationship between management and the political process can be built.

Management development

Too often the political process is treated as peripheral to management development. Too frequently a management course 'covers' politics in an evening lecture by a councillor. The political process is separated off as a diversion from the main content of the course.

Yet the officers need:

▽   to accept the legitimacy of political control;
▽   to understand the necessity of that control in present local government;
▽   to be sensitive to the politics of the authority;
▽   to be aware of how those politics are changing;
▽   to have an understanding of political structure and of the processes of political decision-making;
▽   to have skills in communication in a political setting;
▽   to be able to adjust working behaviour to different settings;
▽   to understand conventions that can support the political process but do not deny the rights of opposition councillors, and to be prepared to face the dilemmas that can arise;

▽ to be able to adjust to new conventions in the changed reality of the hung authority;
▽ to understand how management approaches that support and respond to the political process can be developed;
▽ to be capable of dealing with the stresses implicit in a political-management system.

The capacity to operate in the changing politics of local government is a prime requirement of the senior officer in local government. It can be improved by management development. Management courses can extend their curriculum of concern. Experience can be planned and used.

Some of the issues that can be covered in training and experience are:

▽ discussing the potential for conflict between professional attitudes and local political choice. What is required is not destruction of those attitudes, but exposure of possible conflicts between those attitudes and a changing politics, so that each individual can consider his or her approach. Officers must confront the legitimacy of politics in local government and its implications for their work;
▽ increasing the political sensitivity of the officer. This can for example be achieved by analysis of written reports or video material to highlight for the officer the sensitivities that can be found in apparently neutral statements;
▽ building up knowledge of political structure and political processes. Training material should elaborate, with examples, how political groups and political parties operate, and how decisions are made. It should illustrate the variety of political experience to enable the officer to identify changes as they occur in the authority;
▽ helping the officer to cope with the dilemmas implicit in councillor-officer relations. Discussion of case studies and exercises in role playing can prepare the officer for issues that have to be faced;
▽ improving skills in communication across the officer-councillor divide. Communication skills can be taught, but it is important that the skills are related to the political setting of local government;
▽ developing management approaches to support and respond to the political process. Exercises can be planned to enable course members to work on these issues. Thus a course exercise on the way a manifesto should be responded to can be a challenge to officers to develop management in a political setting;
▽ studying political material, including manifestos, and analysing their management implications.

Conclusion

To understand management in local government, it is necessary to understand the politics of local government, both as it is and as it changes. Management has itself to be grounded in that understanding. The alternative is frustration for both councillors and officers alike, and that can only make for ineffective management and management that denies the role of local government as a political institution.

Using this chapter

This chapter should be used to give understanding of the changing nature of politics in local government and of the implications for management. Those using the chapter can reinforce that understanding by the following exercises:

1   The politics of local government are changing. Some of those changes are set out starting at A on page 12.
   How many of those changes have taken place in your authority?
   What other changes have taken place?
   Why have these changes taken place?
   If you are unable to answer these questions, consider why that is.

2   These changes have implications for management. Do you agree with the proposition:
   The management of local government has to support and express the legitimate political process?
   What are your reasons for agreeing or disagreeing?

3   A changed politics has implications for management, which are discussed in the chapter. The requirements from the officer structure are set out at B on page 18.
   Do you agree with those requirements?
   Would you add any requirements?

3 Management in the growing world of public protest

Key points

▲ *Public protest is a condition of local government that is growing.*
▲ *The management of public protest is a necessary task for many in local government.*
▲ *The effective management of public protest requires acceptance of its legitimacy and understanding of its rationale.*
▲ *An appreciation of the strategy and tactics of protest is required, for without it the professional officer can be the amateur in the world of protest.*
▲ *But at the heart of the management of protest lie listening and learning — and they are the most difficult to achieve.*

The growth of public protest

'No school can be closed or road built without public protest.'
'Once it was possible to achieve something, now there are only endless public meetings.'
'All we want to do is get on with the job, but all our time is spent in overcoming public opposition.'
'The outspoken few can always get their way against the silent majority.'
'Vested interests against the public interest.'

All this and more has been said about the growth of public protest, when compared by local government officers with a perceived golden age, in which action could be taken.

'At least then we were able to get on with the job.'
'We may have made mistakes, but at least we did something.'

As officers look back on that period in the fifties and sixties when town centres were demolished, inner city areas cleared, high rise flats built, motorways constructed, housing estates laid out, there is an ambiguity of recollection. There is a recognition that while achievement was possible, all was not well. Mistakes were made. 'Perhaps the public did not protest enough.'

Now many officers consider that protest has grown too great. When a school is proposed for closure; a secondary reorganisation scheme is put forward; the council closes a nursery school on financial grounds; a hostel for the mentally subnormal is planned in a residential area; a council considers stopping school meals; a council disposes of playing fields as surplus to requirements; a new motorway is proposed; and on many other such occasions, a storm of protest arises. Protest can be directed against inaction as well as against action. Tenants can demand better repairs. Parents can demand better facilities in schools. There is a protest of demand as well as a protest of opposition. Both are found in the politics of the community.

Leaflets can be issued; petitions can be organised; marches can be held; councillors can be lobbied; MPs can be activated; protest meetings can be held; roads can be blocked in protest; the full range of appeals to ministers and the courts can be used. There are many well developed strategies and tactics of protest. Faced with protest, proposals may well be withdrawn by councillors sensitive to public pressure.

The legitimacy of public protest

The local authority is part of the public domain. It gains its authority through the electoral process, but that process cannot be isolated from the politics of the community. In the public domain, the authority's activities are subject to comment, demand, pressure and protest. The public's views are expressed in many ways and in many differing tones. That is part of the political process, which cannot be kept enclosed within the safe procedures of the council.

The many voices of the public are part of public accountability, even when roused in strong and strident protest. This is a necessary condition of the public domain. A live and active politics of the community strengthens local government. Local government operates in the marketplace of local politics and that permits many voices. The voices of pressure and protest are part of the process by which a local authority governs and is governed. A local authority that governed a silent community would find its task apparently easier, but would in reality be weaker as a consequence. The politics of party would lack the politics of the community, and the politics of party learns by a politics of the community.

The local authority manager can easily see comment and criticism or pressure and protest as creating interference with real work. If, however, the managers recognise their role as working in a political institution, then the many voices of the public are part of that institution. Those voices are not an interference with the management task. Hearing, listening and responding to those voices is itself part of management in local government. That does not mean that the authority must concede whenever voices are raised in protest. On any issue there may be many interests involved and the narrower interests may be expressed most forcibly. The local authority must itself make the choice. The politics of protest have to be judged by elected councillors. The local authority has to be prepared to resist public protest, if that is the judgment. Nevertheless the responsibility to hear, to listen and to respond whether in action or in argument remains.

The problems of public protest

A distinction is drawn in this chapter between pressure and protest and it is the latter which is its concern. Both are part of the work of the local government officer. Many groups, whether formally organised on a continuing basis, such as a chamber of commerce, a trade union, or a residents association, or brought together for a particular purpose (often to demand or resist a specific proposal) seek to influence the local authority, putting forward views at meetings or in correspondence. Pressure can become protest when the group considers strongly held views to be wrongly resisted by the local authority and finds it necessary to campaign actively and publicly.

While officers recognise the right of protest, there is a feeling among many that the process has gone too far. Many problems have been identified:

<table>
<tr><td>A</td><td>▽</td><td>dealing with public protest is time consuming, taking the officers away from 'their real work';</td></tr>
</table>

▽ handling public protest can be a stressful experience. Officers who genuinely believe that they are acting in the best interests of the community may be badly shaken at meetings by verbal attacks on their views. To the inexperienced officer — and sometimes to the experienced officer — it can be a disturbing ordeal;

▽ the officers called upon to deal with public protest may be inadequately prepared for public speaking and public presentation. Their style of presentation may even provoke protest, rather than lessen it;

▽ the material prepared by local authorities outlining their proposals often appears inadequate and there is a recognised need for skills in the preparation of such material;

▽ the local authority may lack skills to match those displayed by groups mounting campaigns in some authorities. 'They have become experts, while we remain amateurs';

▽ protest can deter councils from carrying out their policies. 'The interests of the minority outweigh the interests of the majority.' 'An articulate few can override wider community interests';

▽ protest by the articulate and experienced is more often effective than protest by the deprived. Such protest can, if influential, distort priorities against the needy;

▽ there are issues about the roles of councillors and officers in dealing with public protest, and in speaking at public meetings in defence of the council's policy. 'Who should speak? The councillor who has decided the policy or the officer who knows the detail?';

▽ there are issues about the right of employees of the council to take part in and even assist public protest. Teachers have organised protests against school closures and social workers protest against cuts in expenditure.

The management of public protest

The management of public protest requires:

Attitudes
▽ an acceptance of the legitimacy of public protest as a necessary condition of activity in the public domain;
▽ an understanding of the growth of public protest;
▽ a positive approach to the management of protest based on that acceptance and that understanding.

Strategy and tactics
▽ an understanding of the strategy and tactics of public protest;
▽ an appreciation of the strategy and tactics available to a local authority in response;
▽ skills in dealing with public protest and in public presentation.

Listening and learning
▽   an ability to hear, to listen and to understand the many voices of public protest;
▽   the calmness to learn and the capacity to work under the stresses of public protest;
▽   the ability to analyse the nature, causes and purposes of protest.

Management attitudes to public protest

Public protest is a legitimate part of the democratic process that has to be accepted by all who work in the public domain. That does not mean that a council should necessarily act in response to protest. Protest is legitimate, but protest is not necessarily justified. There are situations in which protest should lead to change, but there are equally situations in which protest has to be resisted. A council has to weigh the nature and the depth of the protest and the issues involved.

Councils and councillors will differ in their attitudes towards protest and towards the groups protesting.

'They are merely a group of left-wing trouble-makers.'

'They are the well-off protecting their own.'

Although attitudes to protest and to a particular protest can and should vary, none of this challenges the legitimacy of public protest. If protest is legitimate and protest is growing, then it is important to understand the reasons.

B
▽   Is public protest growing and in what terms and amongst what sectors?
▽   Is there a decline in public acceptance of the activities of government?
▽   Does that decline in acceptance reflect the spread of education and the impact of the media?
▽   Is it a product of a change from growth to constraint and the inability to meet public aspiration by growth in public expenditure?
▽   Has a concern for the environment and a now 'green' perspective led to an increase in public protest?
▽   Do the high flats symbolise public failure?
▽   Does the style of local authority working encourage protest in frustration?
▽   Is protest seen as the only effective way to influence an 'enclosed bureaucracy'?
▽   Is professional authority less readily accepted, and is this a reaction to the unresponsiveness of the past?
▽   Are larger local authorities perceived as more remote, and public concern required therefore to show itself through the stronger voice of protest?

Such questions provide the start for learning. In any local authority these issues merit consideration. From such questions the local authority can learn not merely about the nature of protest, but about its own management, its own policies and its own style of working.

Learning is at the heart of the management of protest. From learning a management approach develops. An authority needs to consider whether:

C
▽   The local authority is doing enough to anticipate public protest? Does the local authority consult enough? Has the local authority done enough to allow time and space for public expression of views, short of protest? Does it take

sufficient account of these views? Does the local authority explain its policies and proposals adequately?

▽ The local authority's policy-making and management is sufficiently responsive? Does the local authority impose its own definition of needs? Does the local authority take account of differing needs? Does it take sufficient account of people's own perception of their needs?

▽ The local authority's ways of presenting its policies show understanding of those to whom they are presented? Does the local authority provoke protest by lack of explanation? Or is the explanation relevant to people's perceptions of the issues involved?

▽ Its reaction to public protest is too negative or too positive? Does the authority retreat too readily or does it resist automatically? Does the authority respond in different ways on different types of issues or to different groups and why?

▽ The local authority has considered its approach to the handling of protest? Has it sufficient understanding of the strategy and tactics of protest? Does the authority's own strategy and tactics require reconsideration?

Many of the issues can only be resolved by councillors. They are issues on which officers must, however, advise. They are issues that are too rarely discussed. Yet that discussion is necessary to the management of protest and that discussion is best carried out in reflection on past protest, rather than in over hasty response to immediate protest.

The strategy and tactics of protest and response

There are many strategies and tactics of public protest and skills that can be deployed. Protest groups can learn from each other. Some protest groups are linked in authority-wide or national organisations. There are national pressure groups concerned with:

▽ environmental issues
▽ the advancement of education
▽ animal welfare
▽ ratepayers' interests
▽ claimants' rights
▽ civil liberties

as well as the established organisations representing industry, commerce and trade unions.

The effective protest group understands the need for:

▽ assessing the moment when protest is likely to be effective;
▽ working out the role of different forms of protest (petitions, marches, meetings, demonstrations);
▽ using skills in publicity material and presentation;
▽ contact with the media;
▽ effective presentation at meetings;
▽ the use of appeals to the minister and to the courts;
▽ forming alliances and widening support.

Not all protest campaigns involve the experienced or the skilled. Indeed those with the deepest grievances or the most justifiable campaign may be the least effective in presentation. Many who have to protest may be relatively unorganised and inexperienced.

Management in local authorities needs understanding of the range of protest campaigns and the ability to assess them. It needs understanding of the strategy and the tactics of protest. An aid to that understanding is the preparation of documentation packages on particular protest campaigns that have taken place in the authority. This can be a valuable exercise in its own right, assisting the appraisal of public protest, stimulating an authority to learning and providing a basis for a review of the authority's approach to protest.

The preparation of documentation packages and their discussion with those involved, ideally both within and outside the authority, can be a valuable exercise in management development for those who undertake it. The preparation of such a protest package could even constitute a project on a management development programme. The material produced will also provide the basis for exercises on courses. Protest strategies and tactics can be discussed and the case made can be analysed. Representatives of protest groups and councillors supporting and opposing their case can be involved in such exercises.

Strategy and tactics — the authority's response

A local authority has to determine its strategy and tactics towards particular campaigns:

▽   whether to make a response;
▽   whether to modify the authority's position;
▽   whether to seek to turn protest into channels of discussion and consultation;
▽   whether to counter protest by an active campaign to put over the authority's views;
▽   whether such a campaign should be focused on those protesting or whether it should be directed at a wider public;
▽   when to listen and when to act;
▽   whether to seek support from other organisations.

These are issues of strategy and depend, not merely upon an authority's general approach, but upon analysis of the particular protest. The issue may turn upon the relative judgment of the importance of a local or sectional view, strongly expressed in protest, and a wider community view, not articulated by the general public, but believed to be expressed by the authority. That judgment affects not merely the response a local authority has to make but also the choice between making a concession or resisting the campaign. If it is ready to make a concession, it will probably seek to turn the protest campaign into channels of consultation.

If the authority determines to resist the protest and to seek public support for that resistance, then potential support may come from a wider but also more diffuse group. The authority may determine to put its case to the wider public but in doing so has to recognise it cannot hope for the same intensity of support displayed by the opposition to its proposal, which comprises a smaller but directly affected public. That is the strategic dilemma often faced by the authority, which may lead it to adopt a passive stance even in resisting protest.

These strategic issues have to be faced in the management of protest. They are issues for the councillors and there may well be divisions amongst them. There can be divisions between councillors of different parties, but often of more importance will be the division between local councillors, directly affected and even involved in the protest, and the wider body of councillors. Officers must be able to advise councillors generally, while respecting the rights and views of individual councillors.

Management development can play an important part in preparing officers to advise on strategy. They can be assisted to identify the strategic issues and be guided on the alternative approaches. The documentation packs can be used in exercises on courses, in which project groups can prepare advice for councillors. A simulation exercise can be developed by local authorities, based on this material, in which course members take the role of protest groups and council in response.

Those who are called upon to respond to protest also require tactical skills. They may require skills in:

▽   presentation of the authority's case at public meetings;
▽   preparation of leaflets;
▽   handling the media;
▽   behavioural skills that can assist in leading discussion out of protest;
▽   negotiating skills required in detailed discussion;
▽   listening skills in order that what is said in protest may be appreciated in understanding.

Many of these skills will be required by councillors as much as or more than by officers, for it is councillors who have to face the consequences of their decisions. Yet if councillors have to respond to protest, officers too need the skills to assist them.

Examples of developments in the tactics of protest can be drawn from three authorities dealing with the problems of school reorganisation.

Somerset County Council holds public meetings, but has adopted the practice of breaking those meetings into smaller groups to ensure a full discussion, rather than the atmosphere of platform and audience.

Hertfordshire has experimented with a different format for meetings held as part of the process of consultation on school reorganisation. The format is more that of a public inquiry, with the representatives of the authority listening rather than replying beyond the provision of necessary factual information. The aim is to secure that all views are heard and are felt to be heard.

Northamptonshire is seeking to improve the quality of its communications on this issue. Public relations consultants have been used to provide a document to initiate consultation. A local authority can use expertise to improve its communication.

Skills in listening, learning and analysing

Dealing with protest can be a difficult experience for officers, expecially for those attending protest meetings on behalf of the local authorities. It is important that senior officers appreciate the degree of experience of such officers. Officers operating in difficult and stressful situations can and should be prepared for them.

A calmness under protest is not easily attained. Officers need the capacity to listen and to learn, as they need the capacity to analyse the nature and rationale of protest in order to advise councillors. It is not easy for management to hear what is being said in public protest. Protest does not speak in the language of the organisation. Protest can be forceful and strident and the very forcefulness may conceal from management the reality of the grievance. Those officers who confront protest are normally themselves involved in the issue and it is hard to listen and to learn when involved. Much can be learnt from protest by those who can hear. Because protest can challenge established organisational assumptions, it is hard for the involved to hear, but all the more important that they do. A colleague, not so involved, can be a useful guide in listening and learning. The non-involved can listen, where the involved cannot hear.

Yet listening and learning under protest can be developed. Indeed attendance at public meetings and at protest meetings can be an important part of management development. In listening to the community in protest, the manager learns.

Over and above listening and learning, officers need the capacity to analyse protest. This requires calmness in reflection. Analysis can cover:

∇ the sections of the public protesting and the sections of the public not protesting;
∇ the sections of the public affected by the issue and their relationship to protest;
∇ gainers and losers;
∇ the nature of the grievances and their relationship to the authority's position;
∇ assumptions on which the authority's position depends and the extent of challenge to those assumptions;
∇ alternative actions open to the authority and their likely impact.

Conclusions

The lessons of this chapter are contained in three simple propositions. Demand, pressure and protest are a necessary condition of local democracy; the management task of local government must encompass the management of protest; the management of protest is about response as well as resistance and about learning as well as defending. In working through these lessons management faces the special conditions of local government.

Using this chapter

This chapter should be used to help in preparation for the management of protest. The following exercises are suggested.

1 The first step is to consider the range of problems that arise for a local authority in dealing with protest. Some problems are listed at A on page 24.
    Do you agree that these are problems?
    What additional problems do you see?

2 An appreciation of the nature of protest depends upon an understanding of its reasons both in general and in particular.
    Attempt to answer the questions on why protest is growing at B on page 25.
    Analyse a particular experience of protest against an authority's action and consider how far it was created by the approach used by the authority or how far it was in your view inevitable.

3   It is necessary to consider the adequacy of present local authority approaches to public protest. Answer the questions at C on pages 25–26.

4   The overall lessons of the chapter are summed up in the conclusions set out above. Consider whether you agree or disagree with the propositions set out there.

5   Effectiveness in protest depends on understanding. That can be strengthened by:

▽   attending protest meetings to listen and appraise;
▽   studying protest leaflets and preparing replies;
▽   reading local community newspapers and the grassroots press, and analysing the lessons for the authority;
▽   using video material available on protest campaigns to widen experience;
▽   reading the following
　　　— case studies about pressure groups and protest campaigns
　　　— material on campaigns available from national campaigning organisations
　　　— national journals concerned with community action;
▽   talks by and discussions with members of protest groups;
▽   preparation of documentation packs on local protest campaigns; analysis of their strategy and tactics; discussion of the strategy and tactics of the authority's response; role playing and simulation exercises;
▽   incident recording by those engaged in dealing with protest campaigns.

III Government and service

4 A network of government and the management of influence

Key points

▲ *A local authority as local government has a concern for its area that goes beyond the particular services it provides.*

▲ *That concern covers the many agencies that constitute the government of its local area, but which it must seek to influence, for direct action is not within its powers.*

▲ *The management of influence is necessary to the role of local government, but it has its own requirements, and models drawn from the management of action can mislead.*

▲ *Understanding of other organisations is the hard-gained necessity of the management of influence.*

▲ *A local authority has many resources for use in influence, but the strategy and the tactics of their use have to be developed in management. It is no easy task.*

▲ *A local authority cannot act alone in local government; nor can it influence others unless it is ready to be influenced itself.*

A network of government

A local authority can be seen as a convenient unit for the administration of a series of separate services or as an elected body charged not with one purpose, but with many purposes, and with a wide-ranging concern for its area and for those who live within it. It can be seen as local administration or as local government.

A local authority that sees itself as local government must be concerned with the many agencies that play a role in the government of its area. Even a local authority with a restricted conception of its role would have to recognise that many of the services with which it is concerned cannot be provided by the local authority in isolation. They must be provided in collaboration with other agencies. The local authority is set in a network of agencies pursuing related activities. Its role can never be an entirely separate role, but shapes and is shaped by the activities of other agencies.

A complex of public agencies governs our towns and cities; our counties and villages. Local authorities, health authorities, and water authorities can be regarded as agencies of community government, moulding the way of life in local areas. Many other public agencies are involved in the government of an area. The Manpower Services Commission grows in its role. Many of the nationalised industries have a deep impact not merely as producers, but in their service capacity.

Rail, electricity and postal services structure the infrastructure of cities, towns and villages. Central government plays a direct role in the system of community government as well as providing an influence on and through other agencies. The Department of Health and Social Security and other departments provide services directly. The list of public agencies continues with the complex of special purpose agencies and advisory bodies embedded in the system of community government. Many of these bodies, such as the Arts Council or the Sports Council, are bodies whose role may be less in direct service provision than in funding, guiding, and stimulating.

Local authorities are not merely concerned with the network of public agencies. Local authorities have always been concerned with the private sector, but as local authorities have developed an entrepreneurial approach, new patterns of working with the private sector have developed. Equally local authorities have always worked with and through the voluntary sector, but in many cases that has assumed a new importance. The local authority is set in an environment of organisations which can be extended to include the media and the pressure groups that surround the authority.

Local authorities recognise the importance of this environment of organisations. The more an authority sees its role as local government the more important that environment becomes.

The growth of influence

Where a local authority cannot act itself it must influence. The management of influence supports the role of local government.

A local authority that:

A
- ▽ opposes the closure of a local hospital;
- ▽ co-operates on a land reclamation scheme with the National Coal Board;
- ▽ negotiates with the Manpower Services Commission on non-advanced further education;
- ▽ works with British Rail on the re-opening of a local station;
- ▽ negotiates a contribution from the CEGB for a new bridge across a railway to improve access and resolve transport problems;
- ▽ campaigns as Gwynedd County Council has done for the use of the Welsh language by public agencies in its area;
- ▽ brings together a group of organisations interested in the development of a naval heritage area;
- ▽ seeks a co-ordinated approach to coastal protection by different agencies;
- ▽ opposes the closure of a local post office;
- ▽ plans the development of community care with the district health authority;
- ▽ takes part in endless discussions with government departments.

is engaged in the management of influence within the network of public agencies that govern local communities. In addition the management of influence extends to the voluntary sector, to the private sector and within the local authority itself.

The management of influence has always been a part of the management task of local authorities alongside the management of action. Influence is becoming yet more important.

- ▽ The pressure on local government resources, which makes it more important to mobilise the resources of other agencies in meeting community problems.

▽ The problems of a changed and changing society mean that local authorities look increasingly beyond their established functions to issues which they cannot resolve alone.

▽ The fragmentation of community government has grown, creating new needs to look across agencies. The increasing complexity of the government structure places a special responsibility upon local elected authorities to comprehend the interactions of the network of agencies.

An assertive politics extends beyond the immediate services provided to the need to influence other agencies. Councillors as local elected representatives have a concern for their local communities that cannot be confined to organisational boundaries. Many chief executives have seen the building of links with other agencies as critical to their role. Chief officers and senior management generally are increasingly involved in work with other agencies. 'The Changing Face of Bradford' sums up this new emphasis.

'Faced with these trends the Council could decide to manage only those services that still remain under democratic local control. Alternatively it could seek also to influence and involve other organisations to ensure their policies are co-ordinated in the interest of Bradford as a whole.

'This would need a major effort by councillors and officers to understand how those agencies work and to develop better links with them.

'The Council still may be able to make effective decisions in a climate of dwindling resources, but it will need genuinely to share power and responsibility.'

(Bradford, 1984)

Building the management of influence

Management has often been thought of as the management of action. The management task is treated as grounded in the direct provision of services. Yet the management task has always involved influence over the activities of other agencies. It has been too easy to assume that influence just happens or that it is incidental to the work of the local authority. Influence can, however, be worked at and indeed should be worked at, if a local authority is seen not merely as the direct provider of services, but as the centre of a network of agencies.

Thought about the management of influence should not start from assumptions grounded in the management of action. The management of action assumes an organisation that can carry out its tasks directly with clear decision-points and procedures for translating decisions into action. The management of influence is very different from the management of action. It cannot make the same organisational assumptions. The management of influence cannot assume control over the activities to be undertaken. A decision on the action desired by the local authority cannot be translated directly into practice.

Models drawn from the management of action can mislead if applied to the management of influence. A joint plan between health authorities and local authorities is in the domain of the management of influence. Yet the prescriptions of central government have been drawn from the assumptions of the management of action as if separate agencies can be turned into a unitary organisation by the creation of joint committees. The danger of using models drawn from the management of action can be illustrated by the attempts to set up joint planning procedures between local authorities and other agencies as if the separate agencies were a unitary organisation. It was assumed that planning between separate organisations should follow the model of planning for a unitary organisation. It is hardly surprising that so little has emerged from so much of this joint planning. Differing interests, differing roles and differing assumptions rule out such models except in situations of shared assumptions and shared aims. Exercises in joint work between health authorities and local authorities have been most effective when limited objectives have been set. In limited areas, joint planning and joint action may become possible on the basis of shared aims. But in many instances that is not possible. The assumptions of the management of action mislead. The management of influence is required.

From such experience lessons can be drawn. The starting point must be that the management of influence requires from the local authority officer very different attitudes and very different skills from the management of action.

B
▽ The subtlety of suggestion replaces the apparent certainty of decision;
▽ areas of influence replace points of decision;
▽ a capacity for understanding other organisations' culture may be more useful than understanding their structure;
▽ the management of influence does not follow pre-determined paths but rather follows opportunities;
▽ yet there must be a sense of direction, or one is lost.

The management of influence is important in many situations, but this chapter concentrates on its role in relation to other public agencies as an expression of local government.

This chapter will consider how the management of influence can be developed in that context by:
▽ mapping the organisational environment;
▽ understanding the culture and the assumptions of other agencies;
▽ understanding the local authority's own resources;
▽ the strategy of influence;
▽ the tactics of influence;
▽ an organisational framework for managing influence;
▽ learning from influence or lack of influence;
▽ dilemmas of influence.

Mapping the organisational environment

In community government the effective management of influence depends on an understanding of the network of agencies which impact on the life of those who live and work within the area of the authority. The number and the range of such agencies is almost endless, not merely public agencies, but private sector organisations and voluntary bodies. No mapping of the environment can or should ever be complete. The mapping need not be complete, however, to fulfil the purpose of widening perspective.

Such a mapping can be an important management exercise. Limits can be placed on the exercise. The exercise can be limited to:

| C |

   ▽ the public agencies which provide services directly to the area;

   ▽ the 20 (or 30) most important organisations — public and private — in the life of the area;

   ▽ the 20 (or 30) most important organisations — public and private — to the role of the local authority;

   ▽ the organisations with which local authorities are in most frequent contact.

The object is to build an understanding of the complexities of the government of an area, beyond that normally encountered in the working experience of individual officers. That exploration can focus on subject areas in which the management of influence is seen as of particular importance, either because (a) the local authority is concerned to secure action, but has itself only limited powers, as may be the case on economic development; or (b) because the local authority has powers and duties which are closely related to those of other agencies, as in the inter-relationship between health and social services.

Understanding other agencies

Influence depends on understanding. Without understanding, there is likely to be frustration. Local authorities may see other public agencies as unco-operative. It is wise to reflect that to other agencies, the local authority must seem more often an obstacle to be overcome than a partner in the complex task of community government.

The first step to understanding is to appreciate that the actions of other agencies are reasonable when seen from their point of view. It is only when seen from the viewpoint of the local authority that their approach may appear unreasonable. The capacity to grasp the viewpoint of other agencies 'from the inside' as it were, is a necessary step for the management of influence. To understand the agency's viewpoint enables the local authority to anticipate better the reaction to its own proposals and its own activities and to see the reasons for the agency's proposals and activities. Given such understanding, proposals can be formulated to avoid unnecessary rejection.

Such understanding must encompass not merely an agency's formal structure and its role but its culture and its way of life. An agency has its own objectives which it will pursue and its own interests. It has its own values, which should not be challenged unnecessarily. In any agency there is an organisational culture and an organisational way of life. The organisation has its own language. Words do not necessarily mean the same to different agencies. Each agency has its own set of assumptions about the environment and about the relationship of the agency to the environment. Proposals put forward should be designed with an awareness of the agency's language and its set of assumptions.

The best understanding is achieved by working experience. The capacity for influence by a local authority can be improved by extending the working experience of staff. There would be much less need for lengthy discussion on collaboration between health and social services if most directors of social services had career experience in health authorities and, conversely, senior management in health authorities had experience in social services. Career movement can be an important step in staff development generally as well as strengthening the management of influence. Experience is not limited to officers. Councillors can contribute greatly to the understanding of other agencies, drawing on a varied background.

Ignorance has to be recognised and ignorance can only be overcome by effort. Thus local authority staff, who have no experience in working for a health authority, have to recognise the need for organisational understanding if they are to influence the health authority. Three approaches are suggested to develop that understanding.

| D |

1   The first step would be to take an incident in which the relations between a health authority and the local authority had proved especially difficult. Officers would undertake the task of trying to see the experience from the viewpoint of the health authority, if necessary drawing upon staff from the health authority to assist them.

2   A structural analysis could be carried out of differences between the agency and the local authority and the likely effect of those differences on the working of the agency. Thus of a health authority questions could probe:

▽   What difference does an appointed board as opposed to an elected council make to the working of the health authority?
▽   What difference does the different system of financing health authorities make to their working — both for capital and revenue?
▽   What difference does the relationship of health authorities to the Department of Health and Social Security make to their working?
▽   How does the role of the medical profession in health authorities differ from the role of professions in local government and what difference does that make to their working?

From such questions understanding can grow.

3   An analysis of organisational culture can be undertaken proceeding from what is known (the local authority) to what requires to be known (the health authority).

▽   How do the interests of health authorities differ from the interests of local authorities or of particular departments?
▽   How do the key values of health authorities compare with the key values of local authorities?
▽   How will the assumptions about the external environment that are made by health authorities differ from those made by local authorities?
▽   What differences are there in the languages used by the health authorities; what meanings are attached to certain words — 'grants'; 'capital expenditure'; 'community'; 'manager'; 'complaint', and how do they differ from the meanings attached to them by local authorities? What is the significance of 'patient' as opposed to 'client' or 'general manager' as opposed to 'chief executive'?

Each of these approaches could well be applied to other public agencies such as the Manpower Services Commission and to the private sector or voluntary organisations.

The approaches build understanding from the recognition of ignorance. Understanding will not be acquired simply by answering the questions, but in reflection on the nature of the other agencies. The need is to obtain a sense of the way of working of the other agencies. Answers to particular questions give hints. The aim is to understand and that requires a capacity for sensitivity to difference, which can be developed in reflection.

Analysis of resources

Like action, influence depends upon resources but the resources for influence are not necessarily the same as the resources for action. They can include:

▽ *Local authority representatives on other public agencies*
They are a powerful resource for influence, if the local authority is organised to use that resource. Too often these representatives lose their local authority identity in the agendas of the agency.

▽ *The powers of the local authority*
The powers of the local authority can be important to other agencies. At different times and for different agencies a local authority's powers to provide a home help service, to maintain highways, to make a compulsory purchase order, etc. can be important.

▽ *Land and property*
Land and property owned by the local authority can be important to other agencies.

▽ *Information and knowledge*
The local authority is a source of information and knowledge. Work on population projections and on socio-economic trends by a local authority have an interest to many agencies.

▽ *Staff and skills*
The staff and skills of the local authority can be complementary to those of other agencies, as social workers complement health workers.

▽ *The public focus*
A local authority as local government can command attention which brings both benefits and problems for other agencies. Council debate and council inquiries can focus public concern.

▽ *Financial resources*
A local authority may be seeking resources rather than providing them. Yet limited use of its own resources may provide pump-priming to attract further funds.

With any particular agency, the relevant resources for influence will vary. The important step for the local authority is to realise that it has resources for influence. The management of influence requires their mobilisation. Often resources are neglected. Many local authorities have given little consideration to the role of their representatives on outside bodies. The management of influence requires consideration of all resources, so that they can be effectively used.

It is useful in an authority to consider systematically the resources available for influence on a particular agency and whether they have been fully utilised in the past. The aim is to extend perceptions of the resources available. The resources available in a local authority are matched by resources available to other agencies. The management of influence has to take account of those resources as well. The management of influence can be the management of resource exchange, of resource-sharing or of conflict in the use of resources. All require resource awareness.

The strategy of influence

Influence can be planned and influence can be developed. In other words influence can be managed. But it can only be managed if it is systematically thought out. The first thoughts are on strategy and there are many alternative strategies.

| **E** |

▽ *A co-operative strategy*
The emphasis is upon achieving shared aims and sharing resources. It can be expressed in joint planning and joint working groups. Such a strategy requires shared interests and values which are not easily achieved.

▽ *A bargaining strategy*
The emphasis is on negotiation. It can involve the exchange of resources. Such a strategy assumes differing interests and values but also a basis for a negotiated agreement.

▽ *An opposition strategy*
The local authority uses all its available resources to oppose policies pursued by another agency. Such a strategy assumes a basic conflict of interests and values.

▽ *A persuasive strategy*
The local authority seeks to persuade the agency to change policies without modifying its own actions but also without active opposition. It assumes that the interests and values of authority and agency are close though not identical.

▽ *A facilitative strategy*
The local authority uses its resources to assist another agency to achieve its aims. It assumes sympathy with the interests and values of the agency.
Each strategy calls for different skills:

| **F** |

Co-operative strategy (team-building, planning skills);
bargaining strategy (negotiating skills);
opposition strategy (campaigning skills);
persuasive strategy (political skills, communication skills);
facilitative strategy (linkmanship skills, high tolerance).

The tactics for influence

| **G** |

The following propositions stimulate thought on tactics:

▽ *The unacceptable may become acceptable if one finds the right words*
Proposals have been lost because of the language in which they are expressed.

▽ *To influence one must be ready to be influenced*
One can often achieve one's aims, provided one is willing to assist others to achieve their aims.

▽ *Influence looks beyond the time-horizon of action*
Influence is not easily or quickly achieved. Time is required to build understanding and the confidence that comes from understanding. Over-hasty response destroys influence more often than it builds.

▽ *Influence can be a scarce resource*
Influence can be built up by past actions. The influence built up is a resource to be used with care. It can easily be dispersed.

▽ *Influence grows with a willingness to take responsibility for failure, rather than credit for success*

Risk is not easy for a local authority, but a readiness to bear it can be very persuasive.

▽ *Influence cannot overcome too many opponents*
Campaigning against the policy of particular agencies requires allies rather than opponents.

▽ *Cherish organisational allies*
Past co-operation and assistance from other agencies should encourage positive responses to their requests.

These propositions show that influence can be discussed. It does not merely happen.

Organisational framework for the management of influence

A local authority needs organisational structure and procedures that support the management of influence. It is not suggested that the local authority requires a department or section focused on the management of influence! Rather it is suggested that the day-to-day working of the local authority focuses so much on the management of action that the management of influence can be neglected.

The problem is to achieve organisational protection for the management of influence. One way forward lies in policy planning procedures that take account of other agencies. Such procedures cannot plan for other agencies as for the work of the authority. Policy planning for influence puts up markers for attention rather than fixed aims.

Other procedures can focus on the complex of agencies and the management of influence.

▽ procedures for reporting back by representative on outside bodies;
▽ State of the County or State of the District Debate in full council, focusing attention beyond the activities of the authority;
▽ community reports, highlighting key issues for all agencies concerned with the local community;
▽ advisory committees concerned with key issues;
▽ job exchange policies with other agencies;
▽ resource inventories showing property and land held by different public agencies.

Examples from local authorities include:

▽ Newcastle on Tyne prepared a social audit on the impact of government policy on the residents of the City of Newcastle on Tyne. 'Social audits emerged as a tool of analysis in the late 1970s to evaluate the full impact of one-off events and the true costs and benefits of decisions. Their most frequent use has been to identify the costs of large scale redundancy situations or social losses. No previous attempt has been made to use the social audit method to evaluate the impact of a series of policies on a city as a whole' (Newcastle, 1985).
▽ Clywd County Council, faced with the massive problems caused by the closure of Shotton, drew together many agencies in social and economic programmes (Nott, 1982). They have since worked with Wrexham Maelor and Glyndwr districts and prepared a programme plan for another area of the county (South East Clywd). The three authorities 'agreed to set up a joint

working party, with the broad objective to consider the problems of the area, to identify needs and make positive recommendations as to how to best stimulate the economic regeneration of the area' (Clywd, 1984). Many agencies were involved in this programme which provided a focus for an organisational network.

∇   Suffolk County Council 'set up a group to look at the question of membership of outside bodies and all county councillors were asked about the extent of their involvement'. They found no overall council policy on briefings and reporting back. 'The County Council has now recognised the problem and proposals have been adopted for officers to be nominated as being responsible for briefing and supporting members in this role. A system of annual reporting to committees has been introduced' (LGTB, 1985).

∇   Warwickshire County Council in the 1970s instituted a resource review into land and property owned by any public body in the county with a view to assessing whether the benefits accruing from their use can be improved, preferably at minimum expense (Vereker and Tanner, 1975).

∇   Glennester has shown in research in Wandsworth how a client-based budget could be prepared for the elderly. 'As a result, it is possible for the first time to compare the relative impact of health service and local authority resources being devoted to the elderly' (Glennester, 1983). Information is a key resource in the management of influence.

∇   Oxford City Council has adapted a city health strategy 'to focus on the health needs of the population of Oxford and endeavour to meet those needs within the powers that are available to the Council and through collaborative work with health bodies and the community in general' (Oxford, 1986).

∇   Manchester has prepared a major report on 'Poverty in Manchester' focusing attention on the issue. 'Poverty effects all aspects of life in Manchester' (Manchester, 1986). Manchester has also worked with the Low Pay Unit on the problems of homeworking.

Learning from influence

[H]   All have experience of influence. One influences and is influenced. Learning can be developed out of experience. Examples of influence on other organisations can be discussed in failure and in success. The district council that could not see why a new town corporation due to go out of existence would not agree to give up its functions at an earlier date, did not recognise it was asking the corporation to welcome its own abolition. From its failure it could develop understanding.

From experience one can learn:

What arguments persuade? What proposals encourage response? What events command attention? What behaviour encourages co-operation? From the experience of influencing and being influenced learning can grow. There is the opportunity to analyse unexpected success and unexpected failure and to understand one's own behaviour as one who is influenced.

The dilemmas of influence

The management of influence brings opportunities that are beyond the scope of the management of action, but also brings its own difficulties.

1   *To follow opportunities can lead the authority in the wrong direction*
The management of influence has to see opportunities and to realise them. But to
realise each and every opportunity can run counter to the priorities of the local
authority. In the management of influence, the local authority cannot set its own
terms. The management of influence requires the capacity to distinguish opportunities to be seized from those to be avoided. That implies that the local authority
needs clarity of purpose, and established aims, not necessarily in detail, but in
direction. Without such purpose, the local authority, far from managing influence, can be managed by influence.

2   *Yet the local authority has no monopoly of wisdom*
In the management of influence, the local authority seeks to secure action by other
organisations in accordance with its own purposes. As a multi-purpose agency,
based on local elected authority, it may have confidence in those purposes. Other
agencies have views, knowledge and their own purposes. In influence the authority must be ready to learn. The local authority must be ready to be influenced if it
seeks to influence.

3   *Proper influence must be protected from improper influence*
Influence is an ambiguous word and has been chosen deliberately. The word has
its own warning. Corrupt influence is understood and guarded against but the
building of networks also has dangers. For both sides there must be a benefit from
influence. But proper benefit has to be distinguished from improper pay-off.
Building networks can strengthen the local authority provided they do not
become an 'old boy network'. The dangers are not arguments against the use of
influence. They are arguments for its purposive management. It is the unman-
aged and undiscussed patterns of influence in which danger lies.

    Unless dilemmas are faced, the potential of the management of influence will
not be realised. Frustration follows those who do not see difficulties as well as
benefits.

Conclusion

A local authority cannot act alone in local government. Even in the provision of
particular services it cannot achieve isolation. A local authority must be concerned
with many agencies in local government. Action is not enough. Influence is also
required. That has been recognised by councillors and officers. What has not been
so readily recognised is that management can contribute to the development of
influence as much as to the pursuit of action.

Using this chapter

This chapter can be used to develop an understanding of the role of influence in
the working of local government and an appreciation of how it can be managed.
Those using the chapter can work through a number of exercises.

1   The first step can be to identify the role of influence by drawing up a list of
examples of the use of influence by an authority on the lines set out at A on
page 33.

2   Next it is important to clarify the difference between the management of influence and the management of action by considering the propositions at B on page 35.

Do you agree with them?

Can you add to them?

3   Mapping the organisation's environment is a necessary step in the management of influence and one of the exercises at C on page 36 should be attempted.

4   Organisational understanding is a prerequisite of influence. The approaches set out at D on page 37 can be used to help develop understanding.

5   Development of ideas about strategy can be encouraged by thinking of examples of the strategies listed at E on page 39 and by considering whether the skills required by those strategies are correctly identified at F on page 39.

6   The management of influence calls for tactical understanding of how influence can be developed. Consider the propositions at G on page 39.

Do you agree with them?

Can you add to them?

7   Reflection on experience both of influence and being influenced as suggested at H on page 41 is the best basis on which to develop overall understanding of the management of influence.

5   Service for the public: the management challenge

Key points

▲ *A local authority should provide service* for *the public not* to *the public. In that simple statement lies a challenge to past and present working.*

▲ *A local authority can easily become an enclosed organisation building barriers against the public's demands, views and knowledge.*

▲ *The public service orientation opens up the authority by focusing on the public as much or more than on the organisation.*

▲ *The public service orientation questions practice at many points: access; learning, performance measurement; procedures; for public service is not created at the front line alone. A holistic approach is required.*

▲ *The search for the public service orientation must begin with the staff, but many of the answers will only be found from the public themselves.*

Introduction

It is easy to take for granted that local authorities provide public services. A public service can easily become service *to* the public rather than *for* the public. The organisation knows best. The public service orientation stresses that services are only of real value if they are of value to those for whom they are provided.

A local authority that puts service for the public first would stress:

A
▽ closeness to the customer and citizen;
▽ listening to the public;
▽ access for the public;
▽ seeing service from the public's point of view;
▽ seeking out views, suggestions and complaints;
▽ the public's right to know;
▽ quality of service;
▽ the public as the test of quality.

The enclosed local authority: barriers to be overcome

B One must start with what one has. In building the public service orientation, we have to look realistically at the organisation. In the procedures of a local authority a sense of purpose can be lost. In the agenda of a committee the public can be forgotten. Many tiers in the hierarchy separate chief officer from field worker. The staff can be isolated in their role. The authority protects its boundaries, and de-

partments and sections protect their boundaries. The enclosed local authority has
to be challenged.

The barriers to access

How far do the public have to travel to obtain service?

Do they have to overcome organisational distance as well as geographical
distance?

How easy do they find access, when they have reached the offices of the
authority?

Those inside the local authority cannot easily answer these questions. Because they are inside the authority, they have access. They cannot easily know
what the authority looks like to those outside.

Distance to the offices is important, particularly for those who do not have the
ready mobility of the car. But it is not mere geographical distance that matters;
authorities create their own organisational boundaries which maintain distance.
The titles of departments are not self-explanatory. It is by no means self evident
that a County Surveyor's Department deals with roads or an Environmental
Health Officer deals with pest control (or even what pest control covers). Few re-
ally understand how functions are divided between county and district. There is
no guarantee that the right office is easily found.

And even when found, it is not always easily entered. A perceptive and self-
critical report by Warwickshire County Council argues:

> 'However, many of those consulted recognised the awesome obstacle
> that the steps of Shire Hall may present to many of the population who
> would find a journey into the dark reception area to be greeted by a uni-
> formed, albeit pleasant, custodian a daunting experience.'
>
> (Warwickshire, 1982)

Even at the reception point there can be barriers. The same report points out:

> 'There is a tendency in all County Offices to barricade reception staff be-
> hind sliding screens through which contact is made by a bell or knock.
> The client remains cut off and his access to the hallowed ground beyond
> is controlled by the sliding screen which has all the charity of a guil-
> lotine.'
>
> (Warwickshire, 1982)

These issues arise not merely in central offices. They can arise in a school.
The Hargreaves Report for the ILEA on Improving Secondary Schools argues
that:

> 'To many parents the school is a rather forbidding place. Teachers, who
> spend so much time in the school, do not always take account of this.
> There may be no physical barrier between the school and its surrounding
> community, but there is often a psychological barrier which needs to be
> broken down. Many schools have several entrances, all of which are kept
> locked because they have suffered from the disruptive attentions of in-
> truders. It is not always clear which is the main entrance. Very few ILEA
> secondary schools have a welcome sign at the door. Once inside the
> school, many parents are confused about what precisely they should do

next, especially if they have not visited recently. Often there are no signs to the general office. These are small matters, but they are important to many, especially working class parents.

'Most of the Committee were strangers to the 61 schools we visited but only in some was entry into the school easily negotiated and in most we did not feel welcome until we met somebody.'

(ILEA, 1984)

Of course many councils including Warwickshire and the ILEA have done much to improve their reception arrangements. Yet some improvements when seen from the viewpoint of the authority may not be improvements when seen from the viewpoint of the customer or citizen. Reception arrangements can only be adequately appraised by the public — and the same is true of letters, forms and notices. The written word can only be appraised by those who read and understand or fail to understand. Working practices that seem normal to those used to them can deter those not so used to them. Silence in a library may seem natural to a librarian but daunting to the occasional user.

It can also be asked what are the consequences of offices being open to the public only from nine to five on weekdays. Should that be regarded as a time barrier that has at least occasionally to be broken?

The staff and the public

Does the authority show to its staff the importance it attaches to service for the public?

A local authority shows the importance it attaches to service for the public in many ways. It shows it by what it says and does not say. It shows it by what it does and does not do. Those who have to deal directly with the public are often the most junior staff in the authority and are treated as such. That shows the staff the weight placed by the authority on service for the public.

It has often been said that 'staff are not told what is expected of them in dealing with the public'. There is too often no guidance on response times or on the priority to be given to complaints. Only if staff know what is expected of them can they be expected to carry it out. More generally, staff may not be told of the importance attached by the authority to service for the public and helped through training to provide it. Lack of training in dealing with the public gives its own message to staff.

The staff are the means by which the authority communicates to the public. The staff are themselves part of the public. If the staff of the authority understood and appreciated the work of the authority, then the local authority would have little difficulty with public relations. Staff who understood what the local authority could do and did would be much better placed to give good service for the public. In many authorities it has been said by staff 'the only things we learn about the authority are what the newspapers report'.

Communication is both ways. It is from the front line staff that the back line staff can learn.

'There should be no secrets between front-line and back-line. Until an authority's own front-line staff either know or believe themselves able — and even expected — to find out about the things their customers are asking them about, they cannot make their contributions to the idea of service across the range of counters, desks and telephone lines where they meet the public. How many school secretaries have at least a "key areas" understanding of their authority's education policy? How many street cleaners, verge mowers, refuse removers can share their street knowledge with higher echelon resource distributors? How many cash receipting clerks in housing officers know about the resource distribution difficulties their Housing Committee may be struggling with, even though they are at the receiving end of many of the specific and highly personal consequences? How many main telephone receptionists are asked to present their experiences of the nature and history of phoned-in approaches to the authority with an influential group of councillors and senior officers? How many receptionists are directly quizzed by the Leader and Chief Executive about the pro's and con's of current reception arrangements in the Town Hall?'

(Baddeley and Dawes, 1986)

Only if an authority values its staff is it likely to provide good service for the public. A devalued staff is unlikely to provide value in service.

The substitute for knowledge

Does the authority know what services the public wants from the authority?
Does the authority know what the public thinks of the services provided?

A local authority exists to provide services for the public. Few would deny it. It seems elementary that the local authority should seek to learn the public's views about the services provided for them.

The difficulty is of course that there is not one public, but many views. As an architect put it:

'Any design I produce has to be aimed at pleasing the eventual tenant of the property. I do have to design for that mythical beast "the average tenant" for I never known the actual tenant until completion of the property. Many minor problems might be avoided if we knew the eventual tenants at an earlier date. . . . The quality of service provided can be influenced by having to design for the "average tenant". Who is the "average tenant"? Does he or she exist?'

If he or she does not exist, it is necessary to invent them. Officers form their own picture of the average tenant, the average client or the average member of the public. Such images are built up over time: 'You get to know what the public wants'. Those images are not knowledge, but are a substitute for knowledge. They constitute a barrier to actually finding out the public's views. If one believes one knows, one does not need to learn.

One common problem is that the image is that of the average member of the public. There is a failure to discriminate between different members of the public, different ethnic groups, and different social groups. If some are satisfied with a service, not all may be. If some know about a service, not all know. It may be as important for a library service to know about non-users than users. Youth clubs can too often provide facilities for those who use them, but be failing to meet the needs of others; they have often been biased in favour of males of the ethnic majority.

Assumptions are made as to what the public needs. 'What the public needs' becomes a barrier to finding out what the public wants. Yet what the public wants

is surely relevant to any decision on what the public needs. Any local authority
should at least be prepared to consider that it may be wrong. What is 'good for
people' cannot be decided by the authority alone — and what is good for one per-
son may not be good for others.

The organisation as a barrier

Does the organisational structure help or hinder service for the public?
Does the organisation's procedures help or hinder service for the public?
Organisation can build barriers in many ways:

▽ The tiers in the organisational hierarchies are barriers to communication.
Each tier in the hierarchy that runs from committee and chief officer to those
in direct contact with the public can be a barrier to communication to and
from the public. In some departments there are at least eight levels in the
hierarchy. Each level can sift information and distort learning. Each level in
a hierarchy is a potential point of control limiting the freedom of action of
those lower in the hierarchy. Control is necessary to achieve organisational
purpose, but as control increases purpose can be lost, in detail.

▽ The boundaries between departments and divisions within the department
are not necessarily drawn with an emphasis on service for the public. Often
boundaries are defined more with respect for the requirements of a profession
than the requirements of the customer. A study in Westminster has found
over 20 inspectorate functions in environmental services. They are being reviewed to avoid unnecessary duplication and to ensure better service for the
public.

▽ The central departments have often been structured more as control departments than as support departments whose own customers are the service
departments. An alternative approach is possible. The Director of Finance of
Hammersmith and Fulham has identified three different types of customers
for the department: 'internal to finance — sections providing services to other
sections; to rest of the council — many advisory services; externally to the
public' (Hammersmith and Fulham, 1985). The department has organised
seminars for staff on Marketing Financial Services.

Procedures create barriers to service for the public if they unnecessarily limit
the capacity of staff to respond to the needs of customers and citizens. Some limitation is inevitable. The local authority does not have unlimited resources. The
local authority has policies to be pursued. The issue is not the existence of control
procedures, but the extent to which they prescribe action in unnecessary detail or
limit the capacity of those close to the public to use resources in the most effective
ways, in the pursuit of the authority's policies.

The convenience of ignorance

Does the local authority inform its public or does it wait to be asked?
Does open government mean openness for those who know the way?
Ignorance can be a barrier. The public as citizens has the right to know the
decisions of the local authority and the reason for them. The public as customers
needs to know the services available and its right to receive them. The public can
find out, but that does not necessarily mean that they do find out. There is a world

of difference between being able to find out and knowing. The enclosed organisation lets in those who ask, but does not tell those who do not know to ask. Ignorance is inevitable and the enclosed organisation is grateful.

The enclosed organisation is unlikely to tell the public the standard of service they are entitled to, the choices available, the way to make suggestions, or how to make complaints. Capital projects will be undertaken and there will be no notice issued to explain to the public what is happening — unless statutorily required. Annual reports are issued but only to conform to statutory requirement. The public have a right to know — if they ask; but it is simpler if they do not ask.

Performance as an organisational measure

Does the local authority judge its performance by its internal efficiency or by the quality of service provided?

To the enclosed authority performance can easily become a purely internal matter, measured by the comparative efficiency with which services are carried out. There is a danger that in considering the three E's, it is economy and efficiency that receive the emphasis, rather than effectiveness. It is more common to examine the internal arrangements for vehicle maintenance or the home help service, than public satisfaction with the service received. Number of books issued per member of staff or number of planning applications handled per member of staff are useful indicators for the measurement of workloads or of efficiency, but tell little about the quality of service. The enclosed authority measures performance by the standards of the organisation rather than of the public it serves. In the work of performance review committees, performance is often discussed without any input from the public, as though performance was a purely organisational issue.

The enclosed local authority can be seen in the day to day business of the committee. If one scrutinises agendas it is rare to find time and space provided for discussion of the quality of service provided. The working of the organisation provides the focus for the committee. A committee's agenda is production-centred not marketing-centred.

It is only if performance is judged by the service provided for the public, that an enclosed organisation begins to look outward.

The experience of service

The enclosed organisation is experienced where service is characterised by:

B
- ▽ buildings that do not invite;
- ▽ the unhelpful response on the telephone;
- ▽ the form that is difficult to complete;
- ▽ the time spent waiting;
- ▽ the letter that can only be understood with difficulty;
- ▽ the lack of help given by the reception desk 'because we do not deal with that';
- ▽ staff who only know of their own work;
- ▽ the department that delays a response because 'we have to consult other departments';
- ▽ the lack of explanation as to why an application is refused;
- ▽ the complaint that is only dealt with when raised by a councillor;

▽ the new building for which there is no notice explaining purpose, reason and design.

One should go beyond these symptoms and see the enclosed local authority in the way an organisation does its business. Consider some examples which most will have experienced.

'In most schools most parents attend parents' evenings. In a few schools the number of parents attending, considering the importance teachers attached to these events, is surprisingly low. As we have already noted, it is common for teachers to complain that the parents they most urgently need to meet do not turn up . . . Some parents who are free to come decline to do so. In some cases the parent may be apprehensive about visiting the school. They feel isolated, insecure and self-conscious in a large room with many parents and teachers. They are oppressed by the queues which form in front of each teacher: they are unsure what to say to the teachers.'

(ILEA, 1985)

Even in a parents' evening one can see the enclosed oganisation in the school. The evening is not seen through parents' eyes.

Or take an appointments system in a hospital (and in some local authority departments). The enclosed organisation assumes the convenience of those who work in it is more important than the public, who can only wait.

Or take the building whose problems for the users are only learnt when it is completed, because they were never asked.

Opening up the local authority through the public service orientation

The enclosed local authority creates its own barriers for the public. It is those barriers that are challenged by a public service orientation that looks not inward to the organisation but outward to the public for whom the authority provides its services.

A public service orientation sets service for the public as the key value for the local authority. But values have to be expressed in practice. Ideas gain their impact in action.

Can access be improved?

▽ If the public do not have ready access, they cannot obtain good service.
▽ Access can involve offices and layout but it can also involve guidance to staff.
▽ Access is not merely a question of offices and reception arrangement, the local authority determines access by the letters it sends, the notices it displays and the words it uses.
▽ Improved access is not achieved in any single act or at a single point in time, but has to be sustained.

Walsall and Islington and other authorities have established neighbourhood offices sometimes based on particular services, but sometimes extending over a wider range of services. The aim is to base the office in the neighbourhood and to change the relationship between the office and the public served. However, neighbourhood offices can only be successful if based on changed attitudes to service for the public.

Neighbourhood offices represent one approach to improved access. Westminster is improving customer service by 'one stop shopping' in City Hall. Until recently the public often had to move from floor to floor in seeking service. The one stop shopping provides one point in City Hall where the public can raise issues about any service with which they are concerned. The results are monitored. Each customer can fill in a short form, of which perhaps the key question is about waiting time. All authorities should know how long their customers have to wait.

Ideas that have been developed or proposed in other authorities include:

▽   open days or exhibitions to show the range of services provided;
▽   scrutiny of all material issued by local authorities, as pioneered by Bradford to rid it of 'officialese';
▽   officers provide housing surgeries to deal with complaints and problems, to complement councillor surgeries.
▽   Another authority is establishing a rota so that a 'duty councillor' is available at the town hall for anyone who wishes to consult them.

How can the authority learn the public's views?

▽   The customers and citizens of the authority provide a rich and unused resource for learning.
▽   A local authority that does not ask will only know the views of those who speak out.
▽   Complaints that go unheard, suggestions that go unmade, wishes that are not expressed are a loss to the management of the authority.
▽   The need is for dialogue between an authority and those who use its services.
▽   Learning should not stop, but continue over time.

A number of local authorities (e.g. Richmond, Southwark, Birmingham) have carried out general surveys of public attitudes to the local authority, its level of expenditure and its services. Such surveys have a value in indicating the general public's attitude on such issues as the level of rate increases, the relative importance given to different services and the public's general level of satisfaction. Such surveys give a general background to decision-making in the local authority, but learning requires surveys focused on particular services.

Richmond proposes to obtain information from users by self-completed questionnaires at swimming pools, libraries and day centres, on such issues as why the service is used and views on frequency, quality, speed and convenience. Richmond also proposes to undertake research exercises into 'key client groups who may or may not be actually using the service to assess present and future levels of need' and views on the service received and required (Richmond, 1985).

Surveys are at their most valuable when they can involve the staff of the local authority in dialogue with customers and citizens and when the local authority is itself ready to learn from that dialogue. In a recent book examining the management of private sector service businesses, Normann has argued:

> 'It seems to me that going out to talk to customers in the right frame of mind would usually be more effective than sending out a questionnaire to 10,000.'   (Normann, 1984)

There are many ways of learning. Other examples include:

∇ The local authority which introduced a procedure which surveys systematically staff and public views a year after the completion of any building.
∇ The housing department which brings together housing officers, architects
   and tenants six months after the handing over of a new development.
∇ The suggestion scheme in Gloucestershire libraries where suggestions were
   placed on a board with comments by the librarian. This scheme led to early
   interest, which later faded away, suggesting that approaches to learning from
   the public may need review and change to maintain impact.
∇ The education authority which is considering asking its career officers to
   question students in secondary schools approaching the school leaving age
   about the effectiveness of the education service.
∇ The development of under-fives provision in Camden which has involved
   sets of informal discussion with parents of young children: 'We carried out
   the study by holding a (long) series of 22 group discussions with various
   categories of parents, and with professionals involved with the referral process. The groups were recruited by a professional recruiter, took place either
   in a domestic setting (someone's lounge) or a community hall, contained on
   average six or seven parents and a researcher, were taped, and lasted one and
   a half to two hours; a fairly normal format for this type of research' (Heiser,
   1985).
∇ The chief executive who goes to see at least two people each week who write
   with complaints about the authority.
∇ Oxford City Council has developed a project for tenant participation in the
   design of council houses on an individual basis. Necessarily limited in numbers, what is learnt from this project can inform the whole design process of
   the local authority.
∇ In Halton a key decision in a refurbishment project was to locate 'architec-
   tural and design staff and quantity surveying staff in a converted house on the
   estate'. A major lesson was learned within the organisation. 'Staff found
   themselves employed not just as designers but as negotiators, community
   workers, handymen, community policemen and in many other roles. They
   learned that quite mundane, trival, and ordinary issues were important to
   people and that successful service management is about activity at this level'
   (LGTB, 1986).

Is performance measured by service for the public?

∇ Too many measures of performance focus on workload or output, not on service for the public.
∇ To measure service for the public, it is necessary to go beyond the organisation.
∇ In the end it is only the public for whom the service is provided who can judge
   performance.

The National Consumer Council carried out a project with Cambridgeshire
and Newcastle to derive 'consumer indicators' rather than performance indicators
that merely measure workload or output.

'To give two simple examples; it is easy to record the number of visits
made to a library, or the number of educational talks delivered by trading

standards officers, but much more difficult to say whether people enjoyed their visits or learnt anything from the talks. Quantitative data should, whenever possible, be accompanied by more qualitative performance information. To find out what people think of a service, there is no substitute for asking them, although there is often a need to raise public expectations. In our small survey of public library users in Cambridgeshire, for example, one woman said she was very satisfied with her visit to the library that day, but when asked about her dislikes she commented — apologetically — that she had not found what she was looking for.'

(National Consumer Council, 1985)

A variety of techniques were used; 'group discussions, user surveys, analysis of complaints data, public meetings and so on. In the course of our work we devised and piloted a survey of public library users that could be conducted by consumer groups, and one on services for the under-fives that could be carried out by local authorities. We also devised a simple questionnaire for parents. Group discussions were held among public library users and non-users, and among parents of children under five' (ibid).

The need is for the authority to look outward to the customer and citizen as well as inwards to the organisation. Performance measurement should reflect service as received and not merely service as given.

Do the public know what they are entitled to?

▽   The public are both customers and citizens.
▽   Both as customers and as citizens they are entitled to know the standard of service aimed at by the authority.
▽   Good service has no place for ignorance; the best check on bad service is public knowledge of the standards aimed at.

Too often the public is placed as a supplicant asking for what is theirs of right. The client becomes dependent on the decisions of the local authority. If clients are informed of their rights they have the means to appraise and if necessary challenge the decisions. A local authority that states the standard of service provides itself with a means of monitoring performance.

An authority can state:

▽   expected maximum waiting times in offices;
▽   the length of time to deal with complaints;
▽   the length of time that tenants have to wait for repairs.

Each citizen is entitled to a statement of the service available, the conditions to be met and the standards to be aimed at. Unless the public know what to expect they have no basis for informed comment, suggestion or complaint. Expectations can easily be set too low.

The Director of Social Services of Ealing has written;

'If the staff of old people's homes, for example, think of themselves as running hotels, in business to meet the requirements of residents, they will produce brochures explaining what they have to offer to potential customers and their relations; they will think what they could do to make their establishments more attractive to users by the addition of, say bars serving drinks, more imaginative and varied menus, less regulated regimes and more exciting social programmes, and they will perceive themselves as employed for the greater comfort and convenience of those they care for.'

(Smith, 1985)

Croydon has produced a booklet for parents giving a statement of the educational standards aimed at for children in primary schools. The booklet describes 'what is offered in all our primary schools to every child, and what we expect most of them should know and be able to do when they move on to secondary school at 11' (Croydon, 1985).

The National Council for Voluntary Organisations have advocated that a client has rights:

'to the fullest information about the agency, mutual obligations to those who are going to handle his or her case, the way in which his or her records are to be kept and their confidentiality, and procedures for complaint or withdrawal.'

(NCVO, 1984)

Client, customer and citizen have a right to know.

Do the local authority's procedures encourage service for the public?

▽ Service for the public can only be provided if staff are allowed to provide it.
▽ There are necessary constraints: resources are limited and the local authority's policies have to be carried out.
▽ Over and beyond necessary constraints, controls extend and multiply.
▽ Service for the public demands the review of controls to allow space for responsiveness in action.

The support given to staff and the controls over them determine the quality of service provided. A friendly and helpful manner at the front line does not by itself create better service for the public, unless there is a capacity to deliver that service. The issue is whether sufficient authority is delegated to those on the frontline or close to it. The number of tiers in the organisational hierarchies that separate field staff from the chief officer and committee should be reviewed. In Stockholm housing department tiers in the hierarchy have been reduced from eight to four.

A number of local authorities have reviewed their systems of financial control to encourage managerial responsibility and responsiveness.

Devon County Council is building accountability centres as a way of:

'providing the best and most relevant services to the local community, as efficiently, effectively and economically as possible. . . . The accountability centre should thus be more responsive to community needs and should be able to develop its own culture within which the staff should operate.'

(Devon, 1985)

The aim is to 'improve the motivation and performance of managers' and also to 'make service delivery more sensitive to local needs'.

East Sussex is introducing local management schemes in the social services department to give greater management freedom to deploy resources to meet community problems.

Derbyshire introduced changes in the library service to encourage a client-based approach. In 1980/81 the country's four library divisions were reorganised into two with 15 smaller areas, each of which, in turn, was subdivided into 'satellites'. All librarians in the county are expected to develop contacts in their local 'satellite' community, discover clients' needs and test the service for those needs (National Consumer Council, 1986).

One must ask whether the following help, or hinder, service to the public:

▽   financial control procedures;
▽   establishment control procedures;
▽   departmental, divisional and sectional boundaries;
▽   the role of central support services;
▽   the tiers in the organisational hierarchy and the basis of accountability.

Can committees focus on service for the public?

▽   In the day-to-day working of the committee, service for the public can easily be forgotten.
▽   Discussion in the committee is bounded by the agenda which can be structured more for the organisation than for the needs of the public.
▽   Organisational space and time have to be provided by committees for service for the public.

A committee has its own pattern of working and that pattern is determined by the organisation. If organisational time and space are to be provided for the public service orientation, new procedures will be required which have their own priority. An organisational pause has to be achieved.

Performance review can fulfil that role, provided that performance is not judged from inside the organisation alone. The Policy and Performance Review Committee of the Greater London Council, working with bi-partisan support attempted to provide a new focus on:

quality of service;

effectiveness as well as efficiency;

performance as judged by the public, rather than the organisation (Jones, 1985).

Performance review committees can play a role but it is more important for each committee to set aside organisational time and space for a quality of service review in which the emphasis is upon the public. This can involve:

▽   a special meeting of the committee;
▽   consideration of all indicators of the public's views;
▽   consideration of performance measures, that focus on service for the public;
▽   direct inputs from the public;
▽   suggestions encouraged from staff and public;
▽   an informal setting that encourages discussions and ideas.

How can staff policies build the public service orientation?

▽   Service for the public depends upon the staff of the authority.

▽   The policies and procedures of the authority, consciously or unconsciously, give messages to the staff.
▽   Too often the messages give little encouragement to provide good service for the public.
▽   In training, in staff development, in salaries and conditions, in performance appraisal and in communication, messages can be given and heard.

The local authority must ensure that staff appreciate its commitment to service for the public. Staff are not normally told what is expected of them in dealing with the public.

They are not told:

▽   what priority to give to complaints;
▽   how far they should go out of their way to assist the public;
▽   how far to help with problems that do not fall within their remit.

They may not have the necessary information to provide good service. The first step for staff should be to understand the authority's approach. There is a potential for service for the public waiting to be released. The Wrekin Council has adopted three key values: 'Quality-Care-Fairness'. 'It would be foolish to pretend that the whole organisation is throbbing with the words. We've still got a lot of work to do to ensure that the values are communicated and upheld throughout the organisation. . . . But through our new employees who are increasingly 'brought up' on the values, through our existing employees who are gradually acknowledging the values and through a continuous review of services in terms of the values, the cumulative effects are beginning to show' are the comments of the Chief Executive (LGTB, 1987a).

Some authorities have launched a major programme of training for front-line staff in service for the public. That is valuable, but only as part of a wider strategy. There is nothing more frustrating than for staff on the front-line to be encouraged to provide better service for the public if they do not receive the necessary support from the organisation. Staff training and development must involve the whole organisation. Communication must be both ways — to and from the staff who work with the public.

The public service orientation requires a review of staff policies which can cover:

▽   induction training
▽   management development
▽   specialist training
▽   staff appraisal
▽   conditions of service
▽   consultation procedures
▽   staff suggestions
▽   communications.

The public service orientation should inform all staff policies in the authority. Braintree District Council's action plan for the public service orientation is based on five core values.

We are *customer-orientated*.
We believe in the abilities of the *individual*.
We must be *responsive and responsible*.
We believe in *quality*.
We are *action-oriented* (Braintree, 1987).

The action plan involves many aspects of staff policy (performance appraisal, communication, induction training, specialist training, role of flexi-time etc.).

Conclusion

Each authority has to find its own way to better service. Service days as developed in Sweden and pioneered in the Wrekin District Council in this country can provide directions. A service day can bring together staff from all levels and all departments concerned with a particular service in a setting away from the authority. The focus is improving service. Two key issues are raised:

What are the barriers to better service?
How can service for the public be improved?
The ideas are there within the authority. A service day releases them.
On a service day questions can be asked:

|C|

▽   Do we know enough about what our customers want from our services?
▽   How could we learn more?
▽   Do we know enough about what our customers think about our service?
▽   How could we learn more?
▽   Can we make it easier for customers to use our services?
▽   How could we improve public understanding about our services?
▽   Can we provide more help for those customers who find it hard to use our services?
▽   Can we explain more about the service?
▽   Could we do more to welcome the public and ideas?
▽   Could we improve staff motivation?
▽   Is organisational change needed to improve service
    by delegation
    by decentralisation
    by avoiding over-specialisation?
▽   Can the procedure of the authority be changed to provide more scope for better services?
▽   Could the service provide greater variety to meet differing needs?
▽   Could the public be given more choice?
▽   What could be achieved
    with existing resources
    with fewer resources
    with more resources?

In the end, action is required. A service day should lead to proposals for action. The public service orientation has to be shown in practice. It has to be shown in service for the public; that is an appropriate conclusion for this chapter.

Using this chapter

This chapter provides an understanding of the public service orientation and of its implications for management. Those using the chapter should carry out the following exercises.

1   The characteristics of the public service orientation are set out at A on page 44.
    Do you agree that a local authority should have these characteristics?

What are your immediate thoughts on the implications of these characteristics for management?

2   There are many barriers set up by an enclosed local authority. Some are listed at B on page 44.
     Can you add to the list?
     What creates the barriers?

3   The chapter discussed how the enclosed local authority can be opened up by a public service orientation. Consider the questions set out at C on page 57.
     How would you answer them for a particular service provided by the local authority?

This chapter provides an introduction to the public service orientation. Those who wish to pursue the ideas further should use 'Getting Closer to the Public' (LGTB, 1987a), which contains exercises and examples on the ideas and their application in practice, and guidance on the development of service days.

6 The authority and its citizens

Key points

▲ *The public are customers, but the public are also citizens.*
▲ *The customer is also a citizen. That does not lessen the need for a public service orientation, but deepens it.*
▲ *The concerns of citizens are not however limited to the concerns of customers, and management in local government needs the learning from both.*
▲ *The greatest management challenge of local government is the building of an active citizenship.*

Rediscovering citizenship

One key feature that distinguishes local authorities from private sector organisations is that their public are not merely customers, but also citizens. If they are entitled to respect as customers, they are also entitled to respect as citizens. There is a double obligation on a local authority.

The world citizen is in danger of being a forgotten word and yet it is crucial to local government. What is a citizen? A citizen is a member of a community which governs and is governed by the local authority. A citizen is a part of local government. The citizens vote and it is to citizens to whom the authority is accountable. A citizen has the right to be an active participant in the affairs of local government.

A

Citizens are entitled:

▽ to know the policies of the authority;
▽ to know the decisions of the authority;
▽ to know the reasons for the policies and decisions;
▽ to be able to debate and discuss the issues that the council is considering;
▽ to have their voices heard on issues before the council and on issues which should be before the council;
▽ to have their interests and concerns weighed by the council;
▽ to be involved in the governing of the local community;
▽ to take part in decision-making;
▽ to mould the work of the council;
▽ to judge the work of the council;
▽ to vote.

A citizen is so entitled, but that entitlement is not necessarily realised. Citizenship cannot be denied but citizenship can be active or can be passive. In local authorities citizenship is normally passive. There is no surer indication than the low percentage of those who vote.

Turnout in local elections

Ranking	County Councils in England (1985)	Turnout %	Ranking	Metropolitan Districts (1986)	Turnout %
1	Isle of Wight	48.7	1	Bury	46.9
2	Avon	48.1	2	Wirral	46.5
3	Oxfordshire	45.2	3	Stockport	45.2
37	Staffordshire	36.9	34	Coventry	34.6
38	Humberside	36.7	35	Knowsley	34.3
39	Cleveland	36.5	36	Sandwell	31.6

(Rallings and Thrasher, 1983, 1986)

Local authorities argue that low turnouts are not their responsibility. They may see them as indicating no great dissatisfaction. 'If they don't like what we are doing, they'd certainly vote.' They may see it as indicating a general apathy.

'People are just not interested and there's nothing we can do about it. It's just a fact of life.'

'Look what happens when you call a public meeting. Most people don't go and the few that do are the usual troublemakers.'

'We've tried everything, but people won't respond.'

It is extremely unlikely that the authority has tried everything.

Very few authorities have for example done anything to encourage electoral turnout. It is a strange attitude. Imagine a firm that said the following about the sales of its products:

'People are just not interested and there's nothing we can do about it. It's just a fact of life.'

They would do something about it. They would alter the marketing of their product, its price or its presentation. They would not regard it as 'a fact of life' about which there was nothing to be done. There is no more reason why a local authority has to accept the apathy of its citizens as outside its influence. It has to realise that it may well have created that apathy.

The public service orientation requires that the local authority focuses on the public as citizen as well as on the public as customer. This means that the authority stresses:

▽   that customers are also citizens;
▽   that citizens have concerns about services even when they are not themselves customers;
▽   that through an active citizenship local government achieves its purposes.

The customer is a citizen

Each customer is a citizen. The customer is entitled to good service but the customer as citizen is entitled to more than good service. The customer as citizen need not be a mere passive recipient of service or of lack of service. The citizen has rights as a citizen in the government of the community.

The local authority should show its staff that it regards its clients not merely as customers, but as citizens — as are the staff themselves.

B
∇   The citizen is entitled to respect.
∇   The citizen has the right to know, not merely what the decision is, but why the decision is made.
∇   The citizen is entitled to a clear answer, even if the decision is negative.
∇   The citizen has the right to be heard and to be listened to.
∇   The citizen is entitled to be met with fairness, equity and justice.
∇   The citizen has the right of access of the authority and to those who speak on behalf of the authority.
∇   Citizens have the right to know what services they are entitled to.
∇   Citizens are entitled to know their rights and how they can enforce them.

The rights of the citizen reinforce the values of service for the customer. Concern for the public as citizen deepens and extends the concern for the public as customer. Concern for the customer as citizen requires that:

∇   as part of staff training in the authority it is emphasised that the clients who stand waiting at the reception desk are also citizens and as such they are the people to whom all officers and councillors are ultimately responsible. 'Every customer is an elector.'
∇   that the authority accepts the same obligations in relation to its staff that it expects its staff to show to the public as citizens. Staff cannot explain unless they are given the explanation.

The wide concerns of the citizen

In the public domain it is not merely customers who are interested in the services. All citizens have a potential interest, for those services are provided in their name. The council exercises powers, but is responsible and accountable to the citizens. It exercises powers on their behalf.

Many citizens apart from the direct customers of a service have an interest in that service. The ratepayer has an interest, the public denied a service has an interest, the public affected by the location of a service has an interest. But over and above these particular interests, the citizens have an interest in the good government of their area. They have an interest in:

∇   the services provided
∇   the services not provided
∇   the level of expenditure
∇   the use of resources
∇   the distribution of resources
∇   the use of the powers of the authority.

They have a concern with whatever is done in their name. Each citizen has a right to express her views and to have those views respected and attended to.

Every local authority claims to act in the public interest. In discussions about service for the public it is often argued that the reason the local authority has to determine the nature of the service provided, rather than the customers, is that the local authority is the guardian of the public interest. It may have to impose its views because of the cost of the resources involved. To meet the wishes of one customer could harm others. The local authority may have to control one individual's actions in the interests of public health or of law and order. The authority may wish to bring in major changes in school reorganisation, which although welcomed by some, are resisted by others.

In all these instances, the local authority will argue that it is acting in the wider public interest. It will argue that the electoral process has given it the duty and the right to act on behalf of the public at large. The local authority has to balance the interests of its customers both with each other and with the wider public interest. That is right but it does not mean that it should carry out that role without regard to the views of the public.

To act in the public interest, without regard to the actual views of citizens, is as dangerous as to provide service without regard to the views of customers. The public interest should not be treated as an abstract set of principles, known only to the elected councillor or the professional. Yet too often the phrases

'We are acting in the public interest'

'It is for the public good'

'There is a wider public interest at stake'

are used as reasons for disregarding the public's views. That may be necessary, but how does the authority know what is in the public interest? It will be said that the authority has to make a judgment, but it can be an informed or an ill-informed judgment.

The local authority that seeks to know the views of citizens as well as customers will not rely on one method but on many. There is no one way of learning. Learning can involve:

C

- ▽ the use of surveys of citizen's attitudes, on for example the balance between the level of expenditure and the level of rates;
- ▽ issue identification in which the authority seeks to learn the key issues facing local communities;
- ▽ the state of the authority debate in the council in which the public are invited to take part;
- ▽ issue exploration in which an authority seeks general public views before it reaches decisions on its policy;
- ▽ citizen discussion panels exploring such issues as the future of public transport, community care or the authority's response to unemployment, bringing together the involved and the uninvolved;
- ▽ the use of the referendum or other forms of community polling in which new opportunities will arise as technology advances;
- ▽ the open forum held by the council in different parts of the authority, for questions, comment and discussion;
- ▽ new forms of public meetings transformed from platform and audience into discussion group;
- ▽ 'we want your views' letter campaigns.

Examples of initiatives in local authorities include:

- ▽ A community inquiry by Harlow District Council began with a Community Inquiry Report. 'Who should plan a town anyway? Should it be the experts — or its users? Partnership-community of interest need to be the keynotes and community voice in Harlow's approach to promoting such sharing of ideas. Immediately this raises the question of how a community can have a voice. There are many voices and there is no organisational structure to let them all be heard, let alone resolved. This report can be seen in the context. It marks the attempt to begin a process. It arises from one section of the community only in the voluntary section and within that section it has its limitations. The report must be seen as tentative and interim. It is based on the results of a questionnaire sent to over 300 groups and eliciting responses from over 100 different organisations. As a follow-up to the questionnaire a day seminar was held attended by about 70 interested representatives and individuals' (Harlow, 1986a).

▽ Harlow followed up this with approaches to learning the views of those groups disregarded by the approach. 'However, if this was to be a complete picture of the town, youth would have to be represented and questionnaires would be treated with the same disdain usually reserved for school assemblies.' Young members of staff from the parks department and from the postroom of the Town Hall were recruited to work on the project and the team went out 'to meet young people face to face' (Harlow, 1986b)

▽ Windsor and Maidenhead have issued to every citizen a summary of their Service Development Strategy 'Where we are and where we are going' with a form for feedback (Windsor and Maidenhead, 1986).

▽ Newham formed working parties from the public to look at issues 'affecting a particular group of people whose overall needs may have been otherwise overlooked in the conventional planning process'. Working groups were formed for women; ethnic minorities; the long term unemployed; people who need special care; young people. The working parties' 'most successful methods have been informal discussion groups with small numbers of people (less than 10), sitting around in a relatively relaxed setting such as a youth club, a community room in a school or a community working place' (Bowser, 1986).

▽ Traverse City, Michigan, used a mini computer system to poll city residents on several controversial subjects. The system, named 'Tellus' was set up in a high traffic area at city hall. Citizens were asked to 'take a minute' to express their opinions (Barbour et al., 1984).

▽ City staff in Placentia, California, personally contacted 'every residence and business in the community to collect comments on city services and suggestions for improvement . . . involvement in the project was limited to management, mid-management and professional employees' (Barbour et al., 1984).

Success depends on the authority informing the public not merely on what it is doing, but on

▽ why it is doing it;
▽ the problems it is uncertain how to resolve;
▽ the issues it is considering.

The authority must be prepared to admit that the councillors and officers are puzzled about an issue and need help from the public. The authority can

▽ issue local authority green papers;
▽ go beyond the provision of the Local Government (Access to Information) Act and publicise key papers before council and committees, making copies available in libraries and other points of public access;
▽ use public notices to inform the public about key issues;
▽ use local authority newspapers to present issues before policy is determined.

Any authority that seeks both to inform and to learn from citizens should monitor to whom its messages are going and from whom it is receiving messages. An authority must understand the bias in its channels of communication. If the local authority is failing to communicate with particular social or ethnic groups, then action is required. But good communication cannot be imposed by the authority; it can only be developed through understanding and learning to use the patterns of communication built up by particular communities or groups.

Building an active citizenship

A local authority that focuses on the public as citizens will seek to build an active citizenship. Local government is not justified by apathy but by activity. An authority where less than half the electorate vote is an authority that is failing in that very local democracy which provides the rationale for its existence. Citizenship is more than voting, but if the citizens do not vote, the basic conditions of a representative democracy have not been fulfilled.

D   A local authority can do something — even about voting. The first requirement is to consider it. Each local authority should consider a report on the electoral turnout and should treat it as a measure of its performance in its primary role in achieving an effective local democracy. A local authority needs to learn much more about why so few of its electorate vote. The first step must be to ask. Surveys can be used. It is a difficult area because surveys have shown that more people claim to have voted in local elections than have actually voted. But that very difference highlights an area to explore in group discussions and in other informal ways.

The local authority can encourage voting. It can:

▽   survey its polling stations to determine where and how access can be improved;
▽   institute a registration campaign to increase those eligible to vote;
▽   institute as in Camden a poster campaign directed at increasing turnout, complementing the statutory notices, which could almost be described as antipublicity in their language and style;
▽   discuss with the media how a turnout campaign could be launched.

Such measures should be undertaken with all-party support. Once an authority focuses on turnout, other ideas will be developed. The first requirement is for a local authority to be concerned.

Citizenship is more than voting. The good citizen is concerned with the public affairs of her community beyond the election. What can the authority do to build citizenship? It can:

E   ▽   undertake a fundamental reappraisal of the nature of civics teaching in education;
▽   seek invitations for speakers to lead discussions on community problems at any organisation or group;
▽   assist the excluded, using the approaches of community development;
▽   create new opportunities for involvement through
     — local community forums to which all are able to contribute
     — greater use of user control in the work of the authorities
     — councils and committees held outside the town hall
     — citizens' meetings;

▽   provide training in advocacy for the public as citizen.

Examples:

▽   Middlesbrough is setting up community councils, starting in 11 areas of the town. Chosen largely because of their special needs, the community councils are regular open meetings which are minuted and take place at local venues. Anyone may attend, raise an agenda item, speak to the meeting or raise individual problems with the council (LGTB, 1987b).

▽   Glasgow has been in the forefront in developing housing co-operatives — an example of user control. By the mid-1980s over a dozen fully fledged management co-operatives were operating. Glasgow has taken a further step with its 'community ownership' scheme, in which residents buy their estates from the council with the aid of loans from private sector institutions. Residents would be collectively responsible for running the estate. In that collective responsibility, citizenship can be built.

▽   Medina District Council has public meetings for comment and questions.

Conclusion

A local authority has a role in building an active citizenry as an active citizenry has a responsibility for building local government.

Rarely will the citizens speak with one voice. The views of one group have to be balanced against those of another. The interests of direct customers have to be balanced against the interests of citizens at large. The council is elected to make such judgments.

More than that, the council is elected to give leadership to the local community. A council will have its own purposes for its area, tested through the political process. In pursuing these purposes, it is fulfilling its role of leadership. An argument for an active citizenry is not an argument against a council providing leadership. It is an argument against a council that does not listen. A council should provide leadership, but leaders who do not listen find, in the end, that few follow.

Using this chapter

This chapter is designed to give an understanding of the implications for management in local government of the public not merely as customers but as citizens. Those using the chapter should work through these exercises.

1   The meaning and implications of citizenship can be explored by considering the rights and entitlements of citizens as set out at A on page 59 and B on page 61.

Do you agree with these statements?

Do those statements have implications for management in local government?

2   The chapter sets out some of the implications. You can test out your own views by:

▽   considering the suggestions on how an authority can learn citizens' views at C on page 62.

Which do you agree with?

Do you have any other suggestions?
▽ considering the problem of electoral turnout as set out at D on page 64.
How can an authority improve electoral turnout?
Why have so few authorities considered this issue?

3   Your overall position on these issues should be reviewed. Consider the following propositions:
Local government as local democracy depends upon an active citizenry
Local authorities have a responsibility to build an active citizenry
Do you agree or disagree?
Why do you agree or disagree?

7 The dilemmas of government and service

Key points

▲ *There is a tension between the collective choice of government and the responsiveness of service to the individual.*

▲ *That tension is reflected in deep dilemmas underlying management in local government.*

▲ *There are choices that have to be made and remade between*
    — the public as collective and the public as individual
    — professional knowledge and clients' views
    — the views of the council and the views of the public,
for in these, challenge can always lie.

▲ *There are no simple answers to these questions, only balances to be achieved between conflicting pressures.*

▲ *The nature of management in local government is forged in those pressures.*

Local authority is the elected local government of the area with a wide ranging concern for the problems of that area. A local authority is a provider of service for the public. There can be a tension between the collective choice of government and the responsiveness of service to the individual. The dilemmas created by that tension can be resolved. Local government involves collective choice, but the choice made can be expressed through responsive service. The dilemmas will, however, only be resolved if they are faced in management.

Public services and the political process

Service for the public is provided subject to the political process of the authority. A local authority has limited resources and has to determine how to allocate them. The political process determines not merely the resources available, but the nature of the services to be provided. Policies are laid down setting directions for the authority and its services, the criteria determining access to those services and the method or methods by which they are to be provided. The public service orientation requires that, both in policy formulation and in implementation, those for whom services are provided are not forgotten nor are the citizens to whom accounts are due. Collective processes are not contradicted by individual needs, rather they are informed by them.

But what are the implications of the public service orientation for the political process? Four are paramount. They affect:

▽ policy formulation;

▽   the framework and the nature of service provision;
▽   public accountability and public participation and, as a result
▽   the relationships between councillors, staff and public.

Informing the process of policy formulation

The political process itself provides channels of views and opinions, but they are limited channels. Councillors are, because of their election, entitled to speak as representatives of the public; however, they are not entitled to claim that they automatically know what the public thinks about each of the services provided. From their many contacts with the public they will learn much but not all. Surveys have shown that over three-quarters of the public have never raised an issue with a councillor. Councillors committed to the public service orientation will use their own knowledge, and other knowledge of the public's concerns, but they will also support new ways of learning.

Setting the framework

The political process determines the nature of the services to be provided and the resources available. The necessity of political decision-making does not remove the need for the public service orientation in the operation of the service; rather it strengthens it. Whatever the policy, however great or small the level of resources, the aim can still be the best quality of service achievable.

The idea of the public service orientation has been interpreted by some as little more than asking the public what they want. The answer to such questions is usually 'more', and consequently, the idea is seen as inextricably linked with expanding services. This misses the point. At whatever level services are set and within whatever broad parameters they are being provided, there should be a concern for quality of provision and for the effectiveness of their delivery. Quality and effectiveness are central to providing service for the public.

Better service for the public require:

▽   focus on access (design and location of buildings, information, letters, forms);
▽   attention to customer views and a determination to seek them out;
▽   search for and welcome to suggestions;
▽   priority to complaints;
▽   attention to detail;
▽   explanation for customer and citizen.

These requirements are likely to be realised only if those who deal directly with the public understand the policy they are applying, have a capacity to respond to the public's problems as they are presented, and have organisational support. Policy should not unnecessarily be turned into over-detailed specification, though there will be times when the political requirement for a service has to be specified in detailed rules governing the allocation of a service. A housing allocation, for example, has to follow a rigorous points scheme in order to secure fair and equal treatment.

There may be a need for detailed specification of the nature and condition of a service. But such conditions should be the subject of clear political decisions, made in the full awareness that narrow limits are being set on the capacity of staff to respond to the public's problems. The public service orientation does not resolve the issues of specification against discretion. It requires that the issue of the balance between them is faced.

To set wider limits for the staff who have to deal with the public does not remove the concern of councillors. Councillors are involved with the individual problems of members of the public. They test the performance of the local authority in the complaints they receive. To give wider discretion to staff does not lessen that interest of councillors. The discretion is provided not for its own sake but to give better service for the public in carrying out the policies of the authority. Both service and policy have still to be judged by the councillor, and for the judgment the councillor is accountable.

Distinguishing the contribution of public participation

Public participation is the involvement of the public in the process of decision-making. Often enough involvement is at the level of consultation, rather than as a partnership in decision-making. The public is consulted about proposals for a new town development, for an urban renewal scheme or over a new system of public transport. The decision remains with the local authority which may take more or less account of the process of consultation.

Public participation can go further than consultation. It can go as far as use of a referendum or, on a small scale, the handing over of part of a local authority service to be run by the users of the service, as with tenants' control of estate management or user-control of a sports facility.

Public participation in some of its forms can, however, focus too much on the collective community view with the result that the individual is lost sight of. Views expressed by a few members of the public at a meeting do not always represent the views of customers and citizens. Representatives of tenants, or users engaged in running activities themselves, require a public service orientation for they too can forget the public they represent. It may be argued that they are less likely to do so being close to tenants and users. But such representatives can too readily assume they 'know' because they are tenants and users, yet that may mean only that they know what they themselves want. The public service orientation does not mean the introduction of a particular form of public participation. It does not mean that decisions are removed entirely from either professions or politicians. It does question however, the wisdom of either defining unilaterally what the customers want and need without regard to their views.

The impact on relationships

These issues highlight the triangle of relations between

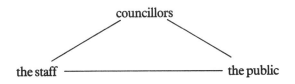

Issues are raised on:

▽   whether the councillors (even with the assistance of the staff) have enough knowledge of, and take sufficient account of, the views of the public both as customers and as citizens;

▽ whether the councillors have allowed sufficient scope and discretion within the limits of their policy requirements for staff to provide good service for the public as customers;

▽ whether the councillors provide both directly and through staff sufficient explanation for public accountability.

Organising for the better service

The staff provide service *to* the public. They do not necessarily provide service *for* the public. At the counter or in the community, the staff can easily be seen as concerned more to impose than to respond. The problem may not lie in the staff but in the organisational conditions. Good service must be provided at the counter or in the street, but good service depends upon organisational support. There are many organisational issues raised by a focus on service for the public:

▽ rules and procedures
▽ hierarchy
▽ professionalism

and the relationships which underpin them.

Procedures may restrict the capacity of staff, professional and non-professional, to provide service for the public. They may limit the capacity to respond to problems and issues as they are presented, but they may be necessary to ensure that the policies laid down by the council are carried out, and be a way of ensuring that limited resources are allocated to those most in need.

Although procedures may be defended and be defensible on these grounds, the justification may be more formal than real. It does not follow that all procedures will be so justified. One test is whether the procedures are seen as fair by most of the public affected by them. Thus, the need for a points allocation system for housing will normally be accepted as fair by applicants for housing even though there may be arguments about the actual system. The existence of rules for the allocation of scarce resources will normally be seen as fair. The existence of rules as such does not prevent good service, provided service carries explanation and the explanations bring general although not universal acceptance of their reasonableness. Rules are justifiable, but they must be justified. Their fairness can be reviewed in public dialogue.

Bureaucracy does not operate by rules alone, but by hierarchy. Cases may have to be referred upwards; virement may be limited. The hierarchy operates not because of rules, but in their absence. Issues are referred up the hierarchy because rules are not laid down. In the eyes of the public it is remote decision-making by 'them'. Lack of discretion at the point of contact or close to the public can limit the capacity for good service.

Many local authority staff are professionals who deal with the public in accordance with their acquired knowledge and skills. The views of the public can be discounted and stress laid on the professional approach as though that were enough. Professionalism can provide service *for* the public, if the public is listened to. If the professional solution is unthinkingly imposed, professionalism merely provides service *to* the public.

Professionalism has come under increasing challenge. On the one hand it is challenged politically, as councillors begin to question the validity of professional judgment. There is a public challenge to the authority for professional decisions. Professional skills and knowledge provide the basis for the professional to make an important contribution, but a contribution which should not be made in isolation. There may be a requirement for new forms of relationships between the professions and public and a new form of professionalism that sees the public not as dependants but as partners.

There is a rationale for the inward or upward looking organisation. Local authority staff, both professional and non-professional, are responsible through the organisational hierarchy to committee and council. They are subject to political control. The necessity of political control can be used to justify rules laid down, limited discretion and the hierarchical control of professionals and others, and yet that political control can easily become a formality rather than a reality.

The public service orientation does not deny the case for rules, professionalism and hierarchy; it challenges their form and practice, requiring justification rather than passive acceptance.

Representative democracy: the need for new relations between politicians, staff and public

Representative democracy can be used to justify organisations that provide service *to* the public rather than *for* the public. Phrases such as 'the committee insist' or 'public accountability requires' can be used to justify the organisation that looks upward through the hierarchy, not outward to the public. Although representative democracy provides a powerful means by which the organisation looks outward to the public, it can lead to an emphasis on the public as an abstraction rather than on actual members of the public.

Too great a burden is being placed on the principle of representative democracy, if it is assumed that through this means alone public service can be secured. Indeed it leads to a burden of hierarchical control. The number of tiers in the hierarchy, the detailed rules, the agenda of decisions can all make service for the public difficult; they can also substitute form for the reality of political control.

The assumption can be too readily made that the primacy of political control based on representative democracy is the only legitimate means of expressing public views. This assumption rules out any role for participative democracy, just as it also leads to an organisational framework that restricts the capacity to build service for the public. Consideration must at least be given to the possibility of the public deciding for themselves: of the collective will being expressed directly instead of indirectly.

The public service orientation demands a new view of the triangle of relationships. Thus, the relationship between staff and public is affected by the relationship between staff and politicians. The issues raised are:

▽   Whether the forms in which policy are expressed prevent or encourage service for the public by the staff?

▽   Whether control systems discourage service for the public without necessarily ensuring control by the political process?

▽   Whether the hierarchies through which political control is expressed cause the organisation to look inwards rather than outward?

▽   What the balance is between the professional's relationship with the politicians and the relationship with the public?

▽   Whether professionalism gets in the way of taking sufficient account of the public as customer and citizen?

It is important to consider not only the pairs of relationships but the set of relationships and to look at them in terms of service for the public. A holistic approach is required.

The dilemmas

The public service orientation raises issues about the role of the local authority and the services it provides. Because it focuses not on the organisation but on the public as customer and citizen, it raises issues that can easily lie hidden in the day-to-day workings of a local authority that believes it acts in the public interest but rarely checks that belief against the reality of members of the public.

There is no easy resolution of the issues raised. There are dilemmas as to the choice to be made between:

▽   the assumed public interest and the expressed public interest;
▽   the public interest in general and the interest of the individual member of the public;
▽   between the public as collective and the public as individual;
▽   between representative democracy and participatory democracy;
▽   between the public as customer and the public as citizen;
▽   between uniformity in policy implementation and responsiveness in practice;
▽   between the use of professional skills and knowledge and the views of the client.

The choices made can and will vary from authority to authority and from circumstance to circumstance. The authority that is committed to better service for the public must be prepared to see these issues raised. The public service orientation does not, for example, demand the rejection of any wider concept of the public interest or of professional judgment, but a recognition that both have to be tested against public views.

A   ▽   In what circumstances, if any, should the authority's view on what the public needs override what the public wants?
▽   Is service *to* the public ever more appropriate than service *for* the public?
▽   Can concern for community views mean neglect of individual views?
▽   Does the principle of representative democracy exclude any development of participatory democracy?
▽   How does the customer of a local authority service differ from the customer of a private firm?
▽   Does the public service orientation challenge or support the political process?
▽   Can the requirements of political control be reconciled with responsiveness to the public?
▽   Are the rights of the public as citizens different from the rights of the public as customers?
▽   Does the duty of councillors to represent the public mean that they speak for the public?
▽   When does the public service orientation deny professionalism and when does professionalism deny the public service orientation?

▽   Should the wider public interest always override the views of individuals?
▽   How far can customer choice be extended for a public service?
▽   Does the fair and impartial implementation of policy prevent responsiveness
to individual needs?

B   Finally, the implications of the public service orientation can be considered
against concrete issues facing the authority. For example:

'One area of the county has always appeared to the chief officers to be
neglected, "almost backwater", lacking many of the facilities of other
areas. The county is considering how transport facilities can be improved
and development undertaken. Yet there is every indication that in that
area the people living there do not seek that development.'

In what circumstances and for what reasons is that development justified?

'Prospective tenants placed high on a council's waiting list have turned
down three offers, which means they no longer have priority.'

Is that rule justified?

Conclusion

The contribution of the public service orientation is to open up an enclosed local
authority and there is no better way to open it up than to question. For management many of the most important questions derive from the collective choice of
government and the responsiveness of service for the public as customer or client.
Perhaps it is through an active citizenship that the authority can seek to resolve the
dilemmas. That is a management challenge.

Using this chapter

This chapter shows that there are dilemmas arising from the tension between the
role of local authorities as government and in service for the public. That is the
special challenge of management in local authorities which has to be understood
by those engaged in it. Those using the chapter should work on the dilemmas by
doing the following exercises.

1   The questions at A on page 72 pose a series of different dilemmas.
How would you answer them?
2   The issues at B on page 73 illustrate the dilemmas in practice.
They can be used to test out your conclusions on the previous exercise.
How would you answer them?
What similar types of issues can you think of?
How should they be dealt with?

IV Applications in understanding

8   The role of the chief executive in local government

Key points

▲   *Understanding has to be tested in application and the first test used is the role of the chief executive in local government.*
▲   *For the chief executive stands at the point of interaction between the politics of local government and the organisation of service provision.*
▲   *The nature of the role lies in the relationships and in that are its ambiguities.*
▲   *The role has to be built and re-built by each chief executive and the starting point is the relationship between the political process and the management process.*
▲   *There is not one role but many roles.*

Introduction

In this book it has been argued that to understand management in local government it is first necessary to understand its special purposes, conditions and tasks. In this part three applications of that understanding are presented. The role of the chief executive, an example of departmental management and the nature of policy discussions are examined to illustrate how that understanding can be used as part of a wider understanding of management. The task is to use the understanding of management in local government not as the whole of the management analysis, but as a crucial part informing and influencing the whole.

The conditions of the role

The role of the chief executive is conditioned by the nature of local authorities. It is conditioned both by the imperative of the political institution constituted for local government and the organisational requirements of service provision. The chief executive is set at the point of inter-relationship between them.

1   *The role of chief executives is better understood by their organisational position than by the activities for which they are responsible*
To understand the role one looks not at the activities for which chief executives are responsible but at their organisational position. Thus the chief executive is:

▽   at the key interface between the staff and the politicians
▽   the head of the council's paid service
▽   an ambassador for the authority.

2   *The role is not determined by the activities but by the relationships*
The chief executive is not normally responsible for particular activities although they may have been added to the role. One cannot describe the role in terms of responsibilities for services. Rather the role is described by relationships. It is in this sense that it can be described as a leadership rather than a managerial role, even though the chief executive has a key concern for the overall management of resources.

3   *The role is therefore made rather than pre-determined and has to be made and re-made as relationships change*
This could be argued to be true of all senior roles in all organisations. But in other roles sets of activities pre-determine the role, at least in part. The holder of such posts has a role apart from the relationship, while to the chief executive the role lies in the relationships. There is no escaping to the routines of on-going activities.

4   *The role has no professional base*
Because there is no responsibility tied to particular sets of activities, there is no — and can be no — particular professional base. That does not mean that in particular periods there may not be a preponderance of chief executives drawn from a particular profession, but it does mean that the role cannot be seen as belonging to a profession. The chief executive seeks definition not through professionalism but by escaping from it.

5   *The role is set at the 'top' of the organisation*
There is no escape.

▽   the chief executive cannot stand aside
▽   it is 'where the buck stops'
▽   crises have to be dealt with
▽   a trouble-shooter is required.

The position can open up possibilities. Issues can be seen from the top of the organisation that cannot be seen from other positions in the organisation. Consequently

▽   horizons can be extended in time and space
▽   overall organisational strengths and weaknesses can be identified
▽   overall political perspectives can be more easily understood.

Although from the top of the organisation the viewpoint is wider, there is much that cannot be seen from that position, and a chief executive's role has to be built in recognition of those limitations as well as of its vantage points.

6   *There is an ambiguity in the authority of the chief executive*
Ambiguity lies in the history of a developing role. The chief executive is the Head of the Council's paid service and as such has authority over the other chief officers and the staff of the council. Ambiguity derives not merely from the history of long-established departments and professions, but is to an extent written into the terms of reference of many chief executives by limitations on the authority of the chief executive on professional matters. That limitation may be seen as necessary, but the very word 'professional' is itself ambiguous. The authority of the chief executive, in practice, can depend upon political authority. In the role's various relationships the chief executive finds and loses authority.

There is an ambiguity in the chief executive's authority, but authority remains. One chief executive writes:

> 'Chief officers have and are expected to have a good deal of autonomy in managing their departments and have therefore only a limited day to day responsibility to the chief executive for corporate matters. The responsibility is in my experience very poorly defined, although most chief executives probably have some authority to instruct chief officers in the final analysis. Whilst I can only recall using the power to instruct on two occasions in more than ten years the fact that it exists is a significant influence on the relationship between chief executive and chief officers.'

The chief executive has an uncertain authority which exists but cannot be used as an accepted routine as a chief officer uses her authority in her department. Yet its existence matters in the relationships that make the role.

Problems or opportunities

It could be argued that the conditions outlined indicate a role grounded in problems. Certainly some have found it so, when first appointed. One chief executive said

> 'I was used to the occasional crisis, but when I was first appointed, the job was the crisis. I was used to a pattern of work, which had its own routines or seasons which marked out the nature of the job. In this new role, I had difficulty finding the job.'

A perceptive American writing of politicians, staff, community groups and the press has said:

> 'What makes public management so hard — and so interesting — is that all these players act simultaneously, with few clear lines of authority, constantly changing public mandates, and frequent turnover of people.'
> (Chase and Reveal, 1983)

Whereas in other roles in local government, there are activities to be managed, routines to be observed, departments to be run, and professions to be expressed, these do not belong to the position of chief executive. The role has to be built and rebuilt through complex relationships.

That is the problem. The opportunity lies first in the very uncertainties of the role. If a role has to be built through relationships, that is an opportunity for those who can so build. If the role is to build bridges, then that is an opportunity for the effective bridge-builder.

The opportunity derives also from the position at 'the top' but yet at the boundary of the organisation. From that position the organisation and its environment can be viewed with a perspective that is not possible from other points. Thus, if relationships can be established, the chief executive is in a position to build a special understanding of the political process. The chief executive can play roles no other officer can play.

Seeking the role

In the preparation of the paper on which this chapter is based, chief executives described their role. Key themes are to be found in these descriptions.

1   *Building the relationship between the political process and the management process*
This is the single most important element in the chief executive's role. The political process and the management process interact at many points, but many of those interactions relate to particular activities or services. The chief executive is concerned with the overall relationship. The chief executive relates to the political leadership and can assist the leadership in giving political direction to the organisation. The personal relationship with the council's leader is particularly important. The chief executive increasingly needs wider relationships to build political understanding. In the hung authority relations with at least three leaders can assume equal importance. The chief executive:

▽   'is an identifiable link between staff as a whole, and the chief officers as a group, and elected members'
▽   'blends political/professional interests'
▽   'has a dual political and managerial role'
▽   'is a "political manager" at the interface between the political and administrative parts of the local authority'
▽   is at 'the middle of the see-saw'
▽   has an 'involvement in implementing political will'
▽   has 'to be aware of the wide gulf of thought between the "professional" and the "elected member"'
▽   is 'at the "interface" not only of members and officials, but also of different political factions'.

The chief executive not only has to build organisational understanding and responsiveness to political purpose, but also has to build political understanding of organisational constraints and opportunities.

2   *Understanding the organisation, realising its strengths and overcoming its weaknesses*
The chief executive, and only the chief executive at officer level, has an oversight of the organisation as a whole. The chief executive has not merely to identify strengths and weaknesses, but to guide the organisation to overcome those weaknesses, while maintaining its strengths. He or she has to ensure that its performance and effectiveness are monitored and necessary action taken. The chief executive:

▽   'is in a unique position to identify and to influence the checks and balances within the authority'
▽   has 'to support a weak chief officer or one who is under particular pressure and also to seek to curb the over-bearing chief officer'
▽   is 'the custodian of the authority's organisation, structure and working methods'
▽   has 'responsibility for smooth running'.

The chief executive is engaged in organisational management, where influence may be more effective than direct action, but where direct action can never be ruled out.

3   *Appreciating policy not in service, but in authority terms*
As a policy adviser to the council, the chief executive has to view policy from a
perspective that differs from that of the department. The importance lies in the
difference. It is not necessarily a better perspective, but it must be a perspective
that is unconstrained by the limits necessarily set by internal organisational boundaries. The chief executive:

▽   has a 'role in overall policy co-ordination'
▽   has a 'particular role in relation to the corporate processes of his authority and
    by that I mean the inter-relationship between policy, finance, manpower,
    geography'
▽   is 'pulling together the threads of policy and control'
▽   knows 'there are areas, resource allocation for example, where the system ex-
    pects a political struggle in which the chief executive and chief officers have
    distinct, often conflicting roles to play'
▽   is 'generalist not specialist but (has a) highly specialised role'
▽   has 'horizons (which) should be unlimited'
▽   'deals in an even-handed manner with competing claims'.

The chief executive brings a corporate perspective to policy advice. That
perspective does not replace the departmental perspective, but enables it to be assessed. The chief executive does not see policy issues more clearly, but does see
them differently. This role is of especial importance where a major issue confronts
the whole authority; the development of equal opportunities and the impact of
competitive tendering are good examples.

4   *The responsibility for resolving the problems that cannot be resolved departmentally*
The chief executive cannot pass problems on. There are responsibilities that cannot be avoided. To the chief executive falls the problems of departmental failure,
chief officer weakness and inter-departmental conflict. To the chief executive
necessarily fall the most difficult problems. The chief executive:

▽   has 'to deal with particular situations such as conflicts between chief officers
    and their departments and to do some fire fighting on some of the major dif-
    ficulties that arise from time to time'
▽   is 'a trouble shooter'
▽   is 'the end of the road'
▽   'must detect weakness or inefficiency in a chief officer and seek to remedy de-
    ficiency'
▽   cannot 'disassociate himself from the problems of another chief officer'
▽   has 'ultimate responsibility for the actions or inactions of the administration
    as a whole'
▽   has 'to get things done . . . in situations where other approaches have failed'.

The chief executive has responsibilities which cannot be escaped from, even
though the chief executive may feel like a 'referee whose decision is never final and
binding'. The decision may not be, but the responsibility is. In that lies the role's
ambiguity.

5   *Understanding the role of the authority in its community and helping it to fulfil that
role*
Most local authorities consider that they have a role in relation to the community
going beyond the particular services provided. Identity is given by area not by ser-

vices. That identity is represented at officer level by the chief executive. The role can help the authority muster public and private resources in the management of influence on behalf of the community. The chief executive:

▽   is 'the upholder of the authority's civic standing'
▽   has 'the responsibility for the council's external relationships'
▽   faces 'the complexity of the network of relationships'
▽   is involved in 'public relations'
▽   has to 'present a positive public profile'.

The chief executive speaks as no other officer can speak for the authority. His or her contacts are not limited by particular services or past activities. He or she has a concern however for the way the authority views and deals with the public as customer and citizen.

6   *Having a sense of direction*
In the crises, in the pressures of political change, and in the conflicts of departmental purpose, the chief executive has to find and sustain direction and to help politicians and staff to find and sustain direction. It is the testing task. It has to be underpinned by an integrity to be maintained throughout the organisation. The chief executive:

▽   has 'a general responsibility for the tone of the organisation'
▽   is there 'to identify the key characteristics of the local authority, its objectives and values'
▽   has 'vision to see the horizon and courage to be at the front leading towards the right part of the horizon'
▽   has 'a vision of the authority as whole'
▽   provides 'leadership of the officer-side of the organisation through the management team and elsewhere'.

The chief executive can easily lose direction. The problem is to find it and to maintain it even in crisis management.

7   *Helping the organisation change in a changing society*
The on-going business of the authority can absorb. The day-to-day requirements create their own stability and easily ensnare even chief officers. The need for organisational change can be overlooked. The chief executive can ensure the authority retains the capacity for organisational change and realises it. The chief executive:

▽   performs a role which 'must mean moving people and events forward to embrace change, develop thinking and ideas, and encourage initiatives'
▽   is 'involved in organisational development, restructuring to meet the changes that the authority faces'.

The management of change and of changing falls to the chief executive.

8   *The head of the council paid service*
The chief executive has an overall responsibility for the staff of the authority. This gives a special role in relation to the chief officers and a responsibility for staff generally. The chief executive is responsible for building a team of chief officers through whose co-operation many aspects of the role can be discharged. The chief executive:

▽   has 'a key contribution in the appointment of all chief officers'
▽   has 'a particular role in relation to the appointment and removal of chief
      officers and in the review of their performance'
▽   is involved in 'getting the best out of people'
▽   carries 'an authority, at the end of the day, over other chief officers . . . to give
      a direction to them'
▽   needs 'to lead the development of managers and management'.

Some merely state the simple fact that the chief executive is the 'head of the
paid staff'. The problem is to find its significance in practice.

Many aspects of the role were identified by the chief executives. Most are
caught in the eight themes described above and most are related to elements in the
role of other chief officers. However, the role of chief executive differs from those
of other chief officers in that:

▽   these elements are all of even greater importance in the role of the chief execu-
      tive than of other chief officers.
▽   these elements constitute the centre of the chief executive role, whereas other
      chief officers have a responsibility for the day-to-day management of their
      services
▽   the role is set at the 'top' of the organisation
▽   the role is necessarily set in a multi-professional context
▽   the chief executive is the point of final resort. When anything goes wrong, it
      is to the chief executive that the members go; the chief executive 'needs to
      know'.

The sources of variation

The greatest sources of variation in the role of the chief executive are the chief
executives themselves. However a number of other sources of potential variation
are identifiable:

▽   variations in the politics of the authority and in the nature of the political
      balance (e.g. a hung authority as opposed to majority control)
▽   variations in the problems faced in the environment of the authority
▽   variations in the size and functions of the authority (e.g. size affects the re-
      lationship between a chief executive and the staff of the authority).

What is important is the need for a chief executive to understand the particular nature of the authority, its problems and its opportunities.

The role of the chief executive relates to these circumstances and to the local
authority's own vision and strategies. Much depends on the culture of the authority. It should not be surprising that there is confusion about 'the role' of a chief
executive when there are wide regional differences of culture and approach, quite
apart from the range of problems which arise from inner city dereliction or rural
depopulation and from particular industrial, commercial and economic circumstances.

The point to draw from this is the need for the chief executive to identify the
key characteristics of the local authority, its objectives and values, and to help
build the organisation needed to achieve and manage change in and for its community. For a newly appointed chief executive understanding is the first requirement.

Conclusion

The position of a chief executive in a local authority is necessarily conditioned by the nature of local government. The political process, the tasks of government, the local community and the services provided condition and rightly condition the role. The chief executive role is set at the point of interaction between the political institution and the organisation for service provision. At that point the special purposes, conditions, and tasks of management in local government should be at their most obvious. But for other roles too those purposes, conditions and tasks are present as well. Understanding gained in considering the chief executive's role has a wider application.

Using this chapter

This chapter is an example of management analysis that takes account of the special purposes, conditions and tasks of local government as well as of other considerations. It should be used to reinforce understanding of the requirements of management in local government. Those using the chapter should carry out the following exercises.

1   How would you expect the role of the chief executive to differ, if at all:
   — in a small district council, in a county and in a metropolitan district
   — in an authority with majority control and in a hung authority?

2   Would you expect the role of the chief executive in an authority to change over time?

3   What would you regard as the key issues for a chief executive when political control changes in the authority?

4   Does the chief executive have a responsibility for sustaining the role of local authorities as local government? If so how should it be discharged?

5   Does the chief executive have a responsibility for sustaining the quality of service provision?

   Understanding can be tested by carrying out an analysis of another role (e.g. Treasurer, Director of Technical Services, Director of Administration, Director of Housing, Chief Education Officer, Director of Social Services).
   Finally you should consider what carrying out these exercises tells you about the special purposes, conditions and tasks of local government.

9   The changing nature of departmental management — an example explored

Key points

▲ *Each department is a part of local government and has to be understood as such, but also through the purposes, conditions and tasks of the services for which it is responsible. The example taken is education.*

▲ *The education department has inherited a powerful tradition of education administration gaining strength from years of growth.*

▲ *But a changing society, a new politics and the changed conditions of constraint have challenged that tradition.*

▲ *The challenge is to build a new management of education, grounded both in the nature of local government and of education in a changing society.*

▲ *A management agenda is proposed, for which the starting point is the building of an organisational culture and that will require a new professionalism and a new management.*

Each department in a local authority is a part of local government. Its management is governed by the special purposes, conditions and tasks of local government but also by the special purposes, conditions and tasks of the service for which it is responsible. The understanding of departmental management must be based on an awareness both of the nature of local government and of the service. As an example of how such understanding can be developed, this chapter is a search for the management of one key department — the education department. The lessons are there for all departments.

The department in its inherited setting

The service and the purpose lies beyond

Beyond the education department lies the service and its purpose. That purpose is not to be found in the department, but in the learning experience that takes place both in the institutions through which the process of education is provided, and beyond those institutions. The purpose is development, whether of child or adult. The role of the department is limited by its powers, but its purposes are almost without bounds.

The education department and the educational establishments

The education authority has the responsibility for the schools and colleges, but it can be responsibility without powers to match. The schools and colleges are separate institutions located far away in both organisational and geographical space from the authority to which they are responsible. They are protected by the professionalism of staff and by the authority of heads and principals and by the power possessed by governing bodies. The relative independence of the institutions is a condition of the management task of local authorities.

The education department as part of local government

The education department is part of a local authority which carries out many functions and provides many services. The local authority is a political institution as is the education committee. The government of education involves value choice both on the relative priorities to be given to education and on the priorities within it. In the government of education the political process is not a constraint, but the means by which societal choice is made. Politics sets both purposes and conditions for education departments.

The education authority in the national system — the elusiveness of power

Above the education authority stands central government and the Department of Education and Science, whose Secretary of State is charged with responsibilities for the education service, but whose powers also do not necessarily match responsibility.

The description of the education service as a national service locally administered hardly caught the complexity of the inter-relationships, since it would have been at least as reasonable to describe the education service as a school or college service occasionally influenced by local authorities or by central government.

Wherever one stands within the network of inter-relationships, power appears limited and, because of that, power is assumed to lie elsewhere. The experienced have realised that while power is limited at any particular point, it is not because power lies at a different point in the system, but because power is diffused. To achieve change has been difficult at any single point. That is not to say that change has been impossible. Power has had to be assembled by influence in interaction; it has not been exercised directly. Change is now on the legislative agenda. New powers are being taken, yet still the system will reflect influence in interaction.

The ambiguity of the management task

The education department carries out a wide variety of tasks. Some of these tasks are carried out in the department while others are carried out in schools, in youth centres, in career centres, in colleges or in homes. Over and above tasks carried out directly, there are a series of activities which influence or support tasks carried out in schools and colleges.

It is hard to give a definition of the management task that both encompasses the variety of activities and yet defines the relationship between the department and the process of education. The management task can be described as the management of the education service, but the range of activities falls far short of what would be required by that definition. Those activities focus more on providing the structure for the education service and on managing the inter-relationships between elements in the structure than on direct management. Where services are managed directly they are often seen as ancillary to the main process of education. If management is seen as the management of action then there is an ambiguity at the heart of the management task of the department.

The tradition of professional administration

Education departments have a powerful inherited tradition of professional administration. Chief education officers and the senior staff of the department were drawn from the teaching profession. The dominant culture of the department is a professional culture, formed by teaching experience. Until recently little emphasis has been laid on the need for specific training for educational administration.

The tradition was grounded in the beliefs and circumstances of the times:

▽ Growth in school population requiring major building programmes with all that is required in administration.
▽ Growth in expenditure on education.
▽ Public aspiration to even better standards reflecting confidence in the process of education.
▽ A consensus on the main purposes of the education system within the many agencies that constituted the education system.
▽ A politics, based largely on a consensus resting on the accepted professional judgment, with party conflict restricted to a limited range of issues.

Against that background the ambiguity of the management task could be overcome by the skilled professional in sensing relationships, in stimulating initiative and in giving leadership in ideas. The tradition achieved much. The professional administrator built the infrastructure for education and provided a leadership to the profession.

The changing world of education

The assumptions that sustained the work of education departments have been challenged over recent years, creating or exposing tensions in their working.

A changing and uncertain society

There are many forces for change in society. The growth of unemployment casts into future society the problems of the present. Forces for economic restructuring require changing skills and changing attitudes. New patterns of social life change societal norms. Recognition grows of the problems and potential of a multi-ethnic society. Discrimination is felt and challenged. New technology brings both problems and opportunities — not least for education itself.

Where change grows, uncertainty grows. Education departments cannot assume stability or that particular changes can lead to stability. The government of education has to ensure that the educational system both creates adaptiveness and is itself adaptable.

From growth to decline in pupil rolls

Growth in pupil rolls provided an engine for growth in education. As the number of children increased, schools had to be built and there was a sense of achievement in their building. The buildings gave expression to ideas of educational change. The task of the education department was the provision of the infrastructure for the growing education system. The department could aspire to educational leadership through growth. Growth turned to decline as pupil rolls began to fall. To an extent growth manages itself but decline has to be managed. Such a statement is an over-simplification. Perhaps it might be nearer the truth to say that in growth specific management tasks are required, whereas decline requires management of the educational system. Resources of staff and of buildings have to be matched to declining rolls. This cannot be carried out at the level of the individual school. A need for system management is being recognised.

From growth to constraint in finance

By the mid 1970s, the world of education had experienced many years of growth. Each year the number of teachers and support staff had increased. Pupil/teacher ratios had improved. Growth in educational expenditure was so obviously 'right'; debate was unnecessary. The management of that growth provided opportunities rather than problems for education departments and was seen as such. It was its own motivation.

From the mid-seventies onward, national economic problems meant that growth turned to constraint or even decline. Local education authorities have had to face demands for reductions in expenditure, whose impact has gone in some authorities beyond the effect of declining rolls. There have been important effects on management:

▽   There has been a need to understand and analyse existing use of resources.
▽   There is a search for performance indicators as well as better financial information.
▽   There has been a greater emphasis on budgetary control to avoid overspending.

Local education authorities have reviewed existing patterns of organisation and ways of working in a search for value for money. Constraint focuses concern for value for money. This focus has been emphasised by the work of the Audit Commission. The Audit Commission has prepared three major reports relating directly to the education service. (Audit Commission 1984, 1985, 1986.) These reports emphasise the management tasks faced by departments. Implicitly and explicitly they argue the case for clearer objectives, better information on performance and costs, analysis of inter-authority comparisons, comparisons between institutions and a management process to use these developments.

From public aspiration to uncertainty

Growth in education and support for its values was sustained not merely by expenditure growth, but by public aspiration. There was confidence in the education service and in its capacity to deliver. Public aspiration has turned into public uncertainty and even public disillusion. The need for and the value of education is not challenged. Rather it is the capacity of the service to deliver that which it had promised. Those who manage the education departments have now to operate in a climate in which dispute and uncertainty have replaced confidence and consensus.

The public of the education authority is not a passive public. In a changing environment, protest grows. Decline and cutback bring protest where growth could bring support. Education authorities have always faced the prospect of public protest against school closures or against reorganisation. But protest has deepened as the need for change grows. The management of protest has become part of the working of the department.

In the past the demands made upon the education system had the simplicity that came from certainty and from consensus. The role of the department was easily defined and easily defended. The formal lines of accountability were clear and sufficient. The demands upon the education service change and grow and with those demands grow new demands for accountability. Management of education departments is subject not merely to the formal bonds of accountability to committee and council. Many forms of account have to be given, if they are to be understood.

The primacy of politics

At one time there was little division between the political parties on educational issues. Consensus sustained the government of education. Even comprehensive education was built by consensus in many authorities. The tradition of professional administration was built on the assumption of a passive politics, which readily accepted the established professional judgment.

In a changing society, politics responds to change more readily than professionalism and has come to challenge that professionalism. From a changing politics comes challenge to accepted practice. Mediated through the political process have come:

▽ demands for a commitment to equal opportunities and a challenge to discrimination;
▽ demands for new forms of accountability for the professions and for the school;
▽ challenge to the assumption that a local authority has itself to provide directly all the services required to support the process of education;
▽ a concern that the curriculum should reflect the changing needs of society;
▽ demands that the education service makes a new contribution to the needs of the young unemployed.

On many of these issues there are of course not merely political priorities, but professional initiatives. There have, however, also been failures to respond to political priorities. The legitimacy of the political process is implicitly if not explicitly denied in such failures.

The educational idea

There is a new turmoil of ideas, developed by the profession, asserted in the political process or pressed from differing sectors of the public. The changes and the challenges of society are being expressed in the world of education:

▽   education as vocational preparation, recognising that may require not par-
    ticular skills and attitudes but a capacity to change;
▽   an emphasis on parental choice and on parental involvement;
▽   the integrated curriculum in which disciplines are linked for common pur-
    poses;
▽   education through life, emphasising that in a changing society learning must
    continue;
▽   education for a multi-ethnic society, with its challenge to the attitudes written
    into past practice;
▽   implementing equal opportunities which brings a similar challenge;

and in many other forms. Management is sterile unless it expresses educational
ideas and purposes.

The education idea reaches across and beyond the particular institution,
extends beyond the timetable and the years of schooling. The demands on management are not merely to support particular units, but to manage a process that
extends beyond past boundaries.

The changing role of central government

Central government has been concerned to enforce change in the educational
system. The dilemma for the Department of Education and Science has been the
lack of the direct means to influence a system characterised by the elusiveness of
power. The means of influence for a period of growth did not carry conviction in
a period of constraint. Controls over capital expenditure had less impact as building programmes were restricted. Policies urged by circular or ministerial speeches
did not result in a ready impact when budgets were constrained.

The Department of Education and Science has sought a greater capacity to
influence the education system through the introduction of educational special
grants and other forms of special grants, by a more active role for Her Majesty's
inspectors, by ministerial initiative and by legislation.

Education departments have been under conflicting pressures from central
government. On the one hand those pressures have been towards a more active
management of the school system, with a concern both for value for money and
quality of performance. At the same time it has seemed that while the changes and
challenges require from education departments a more active management, their
powers have been weakened. Their direct control has been lessened by the new
powers of boards of governors; the growth of specific grants has placed an emphasis on ad hoc bids for funds rather than a development of overall educational
strategies; the growth in the responsibilities of the Manpower Services Commission has made the local authorities dependent on their decisions, adding to the
complexities of the management of influence.

The actions of central government have added new administrative burdens.
The growing range of special grants creates its own administrative burdens. There
has been a tendency for legislation to require from local authority procedures
that add to the burdens of administrative or clerical work. Examples include the
operation of the appeal procedures under the 1980 Act, requirements of school
governing bodies, and statements and review procedures for special education.
Active management becomes more difficult at a time when it is increasingly required. The new legislation on the national curriculum, devolution of budgets,
parental choice and directly maintained schools does not resolve the issues but

rather increases the problem. Education authorities remain responsible for education within their area. Problems that cannot be resolved within the schools will still fall upon them. Yet direct action becomes yet more difficult. The management of influence becomes critical.

These developments do not remove the need for reconsideration of the management of the education department. Rather they make it a necessity.

The workings of the department — problems to be resolved

The departments were built by and for past traditions of professional administration. In changed times, problems are exposed in the workings of the department.

The professional/non-professional divides

There is a dominant group of staff in the education department, as in other departments of the local authority. The dominant professional administrators are drawn from the teaching profession. They hold the senior positions in the department, including most of those at the second or third tier, although it is common for at least one position to be held by an administrative officer or by an accountant.

The professional background of these staff has been seen as giving confidence and support to the teachers as well as bringing valuable and necessary experience. Yet there are many in the department to whom that road is closed. They have not been teachers and will not be. Some belong to other occupational groups, such as careers officers or educational welfare officers with their own career patterns. Others are clerical or administrative officers who have found their career path limited to the one or two senior administrative roles.

In the occupational groups and in the professional/non-professional divide there are potential lines of fissure.

A department in search of a culture

Within the education department, the norms of the teaching profession dominate the departmental culture. The majority of the senior staff come from that profession and identify with it. When the main task of the education department was the management of growth, the dominant culture was expressed in felt achievement. That culture provides little sustenance in an era when the management of education is conditioned by declining resources and declining roles. Nor may it fully meet the needs of a period when education is seen as a process that continues beyond the school. Education departments have to find a new culture that gives expression to emerging concepts of education and involves all the staff of the department. The professional culture of the teacher may by itself no longer help.

The heart of the profession

The profession of educational administrator was based in the school. That was its strength. The strength of the profession was also its weakness. While the professionals had experience of schools, they did not have experience of other aspects of the department's work. Nor did professional training as teachers equip the educational administrators for the work for which they were responsible. The gap between teaching experience and work has been sharpened by new concerns for value for money, for contracting out, reorganisation of ancillary services, for marketing and for industrial relations issues.

A profession reinforces professional solidarity, which can lead to separatism within the authority. There were many early difficulties in education departments adjusting to both corporate management and to strong political leadership. In part this was a reaction to a distorted concept of corporate management as the management of all activities, rather than the identification of key corporate issues. That reinforced separatism. Yet in a changing society many of the issues facing education departments involve other departments and require a response from all departments.

In a changing society there is a challenge to past models of professionalism. It may be that new models of professionalism are required and are being developed based on the continuing need to learn, not least from those whom the professional serves.

An uncertainty of role

At the heart of the work of the education department lies an uncertainty as to its role in present times. That derives in part from the uncertain nature of the relationship between the department and the institutions. The department has inherited sets of administrative and financial controls over the institutions, but limited means of influence over the process of education in those institutions. Indeed in one authority the director said 'we used to give freedom over the curriculum but control the administration in detail. That may be the reverse of what is now required'. In future, new legislation means that there will be a national curriculum and devolution of administrative and financial controls. Uncertainty of role is deepening.

The need for changing staff roles

As the issues facing local education authorities change, various groups of staff in the department have had to reconsider and redefine their roles. In that redefinition continuity with past practice and values has to be combined with adaptability to new needs. There are many examples of such changes. Two are highlighted:

▽ *Careers service*
    The careers service is having to redefine its role in an era of endemic unemployment. It is ceasing to be a placement service, but a counselling and guidance service for the unemployed, moving beyond the schools and building links with the Manpower Services Commission.
▽ *The youth and community service*
    The youth service faces the same challenge in which it has to adapt to new needs. It also has to meet the challenge of widening its approach to meet the needs of young women as well as young men and of the black minority as well as the white majority.

Staff have to be helped to change their role and acquire new skills.

The opportunities and dangers of entrepreneurialism

In the past departments relied on two main sources of finance: rate support grant and rates. Faced with constraint, departments seek other sources of funds. These can come from the present and likely growth of specific grants, from the Manpower Services Commission, from the European Social Fund, from the private sector or from the variety of sources which resourceful departments can find. This has led to a new entrepreneurialism which seeks out funds, seizes opportunities and builds links to obtain resources that would not otherwise be available.

The new entrepreneurialism can create problems. Attention devoted to seeking out resources can be drawn away from attention to the main work of the department. The projects for which it is possible to attract funds may not be the priorities of the department. For some projects the funding is short term so that success can build up long term financial problems.

The demoralised staff

There have always been powerful teacher unions. There were deep discontents that salary did not reflect role. Yet morale drew strength from agreed purposes and public aspiration. The assumption was that the teaching force did not have to be managed. So much has changed — and not merely for the teaching force. The teachers' dispute tells the story not merely of an industrial dispute, but of a demoralised service. Relationships have been harmed in dispute and their rebuilding is a major challenge to management.

Discrimination in the tradition

The tradition of professional administration was built in a society which discriminated on grounds of race and sex and yet denied that discrimination. Professionals themselves reflected that discrimination, even though they were not conscious of it. The senior management of the department is overwhelmingly white and male. A concern for equal opportunities has to be expressed by and through the education service. Institutional discrimination has been inherited. Management has to challenge that discrimination.

The lack of a management approach

The working of the department was deeply influenced by the professional model — the teacher as the individual performer in the classroom. It was the model of the dedicated professionals who were able to get on with their work. It was assumed that the staff of the education department could be relied upon to get on with the work. They did not have to be managed. The world of education has its legendary figures. They were the great performers, stimulating by the excitement of ideas. The chief officer performed and by that performance set a style for the department and, through ideas in action, set directions for the service. The stress was, however, on the individual professional. The professional model appeared to meet the needs of the time. There was no felt need for a management approach. Now that need can be seen. The search for a management model leads to questions:

A   ▽   Is the department an organisation with a shared purpose or a collection of or-
         ganisations with different purposes?
     ▽   Do the staff in the department know what they are trying to achieve?
     ▽   Do staff in the department have a sense of belonging?
     ▽   Is the development of staff seen as a requirement by the department?
     ▽   Are there processes and policies of staff management that can guide the de-
         velopment of staff within the department?
     ▽   Is there an understanding of how activities inter-relate?
     ▽   Is there a shared concept of the management task?
     ▽   Has the department adequate management processes to carry out its task?
     ▽   Has the department adequate management information geared to its manage-
         ment task?
     ▽   Does the department manage the changing of its role and relationships?
     ▽   Do the management processes of the department gain direction from the
         political processes?

Such questions raise the issue of whether the department is managed. The
answer will vary as it has in the past. There are, however, developments taking
place in building approaches to management in education. A few examples must
suffice.

In Lancashire, working groups have been set up to analyse, explore and develop the culture of the department. Working groups have examined: a sense of
belonging; the image of the department; internal communications; external communications. In exploring culture the department has begun to lay the basis of active staff policies. In exploring these previously unexplored areas the working
groups were themselves an innovation in staff communication.

In Cambridgeshire, the department already committed to medium term
financial planning has moved to the preparation of an education service plan,
making clear the issues faced and the aims of the department with an organisational development plan showing what is required of the organisation.

In Croydon, curriculum requirements and agreed level of attainments have
been laid down after widespread consultation. Those policies can become the key
management instrument, providing a basis for evaluation in schools, guiding
staffing policies and informing the budget.

In these and in other authorities management is being developed in the reality
of work in education departments.

The new agenda of management concern

The argument of the paper has been that past traditions of professional administration are no longer an adequate basis for the work of the department. The
changes and challenges faced by the department require a management response
that can still build on those traditions. A management response is required that
realises the collective strength of the department, based on a concept of the management task relating the work of the department to the process of education. A
new agenda of management concern is required and is being developed.

Organisational culture

The issue is whether an organisational culture can be built for present reality.

The education department needs an organisational culture that can give a sense of purpose to those who work within it. If the resources of the department are to be fully developed and utilised there must be shared values reflected in organisational behaviour. Those values must reflect both the values of service and of government in a changing society. At a time of change the education department needs an active culture.

Two barriers stand in its way. The first is recollection of the past, which can undermine the search for new values in the present. The second is divisions within the department. The issue must be whether the dominant organisational culture belongs to the few professionals or to the many staff. Perhaps the issue is whether the culture could even extend beyond the department to the whole service.

Organisational understanding

The issue is whether there is a basis for organisational understanding.

If an organisation is to be changed it has to be managed. If an organisation has to be managed, it has first to be understood. An education department, like any organisation, has its own way of life. It has its culture and its subcultures. It has its divisions and its barriers. It has an inertia that can frustrate and deny change that is alien to that way of life. It has its biases that favour certain groups and discriminate against others. A new culture can only be established in organisational understanding.

The management of communication

The issue is whether new patterns of communication can bridge organisational divides.

An organisational culture must be built through communication, and communication can take many forms. Values are communicated by what is said and by what is not said. Learning is as important as explaining; communication does not necessarily follow hierarchical prescription.

Many means are required: a working group can communicate; a seminar can communicate; training can communicate; a visit can communicate; a staff forum can communicate; interlocking groups can communicate as well as reports, newsletters, circulars. The key lesson is that no single channel of communication is adequate. Each carries its own distortion.

The style of management

The issue is whether new styles are required for changed times.

In changed times the style of management must change. Under challenge staff need support. For change leadership can be important. One can only suggest lines of approach:

▽   There is a greater need for leadership by chief education officers, at a time when the leadership becomes more difficult.
▽   Leadership by chief education officers cannot deny legitimate political direction, but must express it.
▽   The leadership is likely to come from involving and being involved, listening as well as talking, caring as well as directing.

▽   Leadership has to find a style for the times yet each leader must find their own
style.

In a new political world

The issue is how management can encompass political purposes.

The newly emerging management in education has to be grounded in acceptance both of the reality and of the legitimacy of the political process. Management in the education service must be grounded in political purpose. This may require:

▽   greater political sensitivity;
▽   management processes related to political manifestos or policy statements;
▽   joint member officer working parties;
▽   identification of key political concerns (e.g. equal opportunities, community involvement, privatisation), as priorities for management action.

System management

The issue is how to clarify the role of the education department in the management of education.

There has been an ambiguity in the management of education. That ambiguity is being increased, not lessened, by recent legislation. Yet the education department remains responsible for the education system within its area. That requires from the local authority consideration of the means at its disposal to discharge that responsibility.

Four considerations stand out. The education department will require:

▽   clarity as to its task;
▽   procedures for planning programming and performance review to achieve its aims;
▽   the development of the management of influence;
▽   effective use of the resources at its disposal.

The task of the education department is to set conditions for education to achieve purposes formed through the political process.

Contained in this definition of the task is a recognition that the education department is:

▽   concerned with outcomes of education
▽   but cannot often achieve those outcomes directly, but only by setting conditions in which they can be achieved
▽   yet has a responsibility to look beyond particular institutions towards the education system itself.

The issue is how to use the instruments available to achieve those ends.

Planning and programming processes

The issue is whether the department requires new planning and programming processes.

Planning is a requirement for the development of the education service in a period of change. It can provide a sense of direction for the diverse activities of the department and a focus for the management of influence. It can guide resource allocation and provide a basis for inter-departmental co-ordination. It involves the authority making explicit the policies that underlie its actions. Purpose can be rescued from the detail of decisions and can be used to guide the detail rather than be determined by it.

Planning processes must reflect the situation in which they are set. Planning is not for certainty, but to cope with uncertainty. Planning cannot ignore the political process but must express it. Planning cannot presume the possibility of action, where influence is the management approach. The comprehensive planning of the past sought the certainty of administrative action. In the selectivity of purpose new planning processes can meet uncertainty and guide action.

Beyond the direction of planning, programming of action can make explicit the tasks that have to be perfomed within the resources available and against which performance is to be judged. The implicit, by being made explicit, comes within the scope of management.

The management of influence

The issue is whether the education department makes effective use of its means to influence the education service.

The department is engaged more in the management of influence than the management of action over a wide range of its activities. It touches the schools and institutions in many ways and at many points, but it does not continuously manage them. Within acceptance of the quasi-autonomy of the school, the management of influence can be developed.

∇ The many points of influence upon the school are adequately brought together.

∇ The different elements of the education service are adequately linked in influence.

∇ The authority should make clear its educational policies as a basis for influence.

Resource management

The issue is whether the education departments have adequate means to manage resource usage.

Financial pressures have led education departments to consider their approach to resource management. Questions are being raised as to whether:

∇ the long term or short term resource consequences of policy decisions have been fully analysed;

∇ there has been sufficient resource analysis and management of on-going activities — an issue that has to be faced under the impact of competitive tendering;

∇ the way resources have been allocated between different schools has been fair and equitable;

∇ the budgetary processes show the connection between resource allocation decisions and educational outcomes.

Financial devolution does not lessen the need for resource management at the departmental level. It is in over-detailed financial control that resource management is lost.

Performance review

The issue is whether the education service needs processes of performance review and on what principles they should be based.

There are growing demands for the education service to account for its performance. There are questions to be raised as to the form in which the account will be given, by whom it will be given and how it will be evaluated.

▽   Is a new emphasis on performance review required as a basis of accountability?

▽   How is performance to be assessed? What is the role of performance indicators?

▽   Should the emphasis be on professional evaluation within the school itself or is external evaluation required?

▽   What is then the role in performance review of the school, the board of governors, the education committee and the wider community?

▽   Does the education department itself require new processes of performance review?

▽   Are accountabilities sufficiently clear within the department for effective performance review?

Performance review must understand the nature of education. Performance in education has many dimensions. Over-simple performance indicators can distort. The need is to develop the assessment of a multidimensional performance rather than over-reliance on output measures set in a single dimension.

Staff management

The issue is whether education departments should develop active processes of staff management.

Unfairly it could be said that there has been no active tradition of staff management within departments. Yet in a period of change there is a need for increasing emphasis on staff management to:

▽   develop staff for new management processes;
▽   build a new motivation;
▽   build new skills;
▽   develop understanding of departmental purposes.

This raises questions as to whether

▽   the task of staff management is given sufficient recognition;
▽   a new emphasis is required on internal training;
▽   processes of staff development and appraisal are required.

New information requirements

The issue is whether education departments have adequate information for management.

In changing circumstances education departments require new information. That information is being developed in a number of ways:

▽   more information on staffing is being assembled to handle the problems of declining rolls;

▽   more information on the curriculum is required and will be required by the
    national curriculum;
▽   more information is required on services subject to competitive tendering;
▽   performance indicators and other means of assessing performance become
    important;
▽   information on public attitudes is sought.

As the department redefines its management tasks, so does it redefine its requirements for management information.

Towards a new professionalism and a new management

The issue is whether in changed times professionalism itself has to change.
The professionalism of the educational administrator has been a strength, but
in changed times that tradition is no longer enough. The professionalism of the
educational administrator was always a limited professionalism, because it was
based not on their work in the department, but on their background as teachers.
Experience as teachers can be important. That requirement continues virtually
unchallenged. In practical terms that is likely to continue for most senior management but not necessarily for all. A local authority may see the need to bring in new
experience and background. Discrimination may need to be challenged in new
sources of recruitment.
Whatever the starting point, the issue can be raised as to whether that experience is enough. Experience could involve work

▽   in sections of the education departments;
▽   in other departments of local government;
▽   in the Department of Education and Science;
▽   in other parts of the public sector;
▽   in the private sector;
▽   in voluntary organisations;
▽   in educational institutions to update or to widen experience.

If experience is relevant, then wider experience is relevant.
There is, however, a wider challenge to the nature of professionalism itself.
The management of education departments requires more than the professional
tradition. It may require both professional development and management development that will focus on:

▽   the need for continuous learning as management and professionalism change
    to meet the needs of a changing society;
▽   both the requirements of local government and of the education service;
▽   the need to look outward to the public as customer and citizen;
▽   widening experience to ease the building of links across organisational and
    professional boundaries;
▽   the management tasks that are required by the management agenda and the
    skills, attitudes and knowlege they demand.

It may be that a new professionalism will be combined with a new management.

Conclusion

Management must be grounded in the conditions and purposes of the organisation. Management is not a set of ideas that can or should be imposed upon each and any organisation. Management in education departments must meet the special purposes, conditions and tasks both of local government and of the service. That has to be understood not merely of education departments but of all departments. Local authorities are political institutions for local government and organisations providing services for the public.

Using this chapter

This chapter is an example of management analysis of a local government department that takes account of the special purposes, conditions and tasks both of local government and of the service. It should be used to assist in carrying out one's own analyses, reinforcing understanding of the management of local government and of its services.

Those using the chapter should take the management agenda and apply it to a particular department, working through the setting of the department, the changes it faces and the problems in its management as in this chapter.

If it is an education department then the question to answer is 'How does that agenda differ from that proposed in the chapter and why?'

If it is another department then the question to answer is 'How does that agenda differ from that proposed in the chapter for education and why?'

Finally you should consider what carrying out the analysis tells you about the special purposes, conditions and tasks both of management in local government and of the service. In each case the questions at A on page 93 can be asked and added to. The answers will vary from department to department.

10   Grounding policy discussion in the reality of local government

Key points

▲ *Policy discussions provide a window of insight into the nature of management in local government.*

▲ *The folklore of some authorities is that councillors will not discuss policy (in others it is the reverse; they will discuss it endlessly).*

▲ *The truth may be that policy is discussed the only way it can be discussed in local government — but that many do not recognise it.*

▲ *Policy is discussed in informal not in formal settings; policy moves from the general to the particular because that is where it is tested; policy choice normally lies in balance, for government has to weigh both values and interests.*

▲ *To strengthen policy discussion, one must work with the grain. The way policy is discussed is the way policy is discussed. The councillors who discuss policy without appearing to do so may know best.*

Introduction

In this chapter a problem is examined that lies at the heart of local government: policy discussion. In policy discussion, political processes can give management direction. The nature of policy discussion has to take account of the purposes and conditions of local government if it is to be successful. Too often a framework for policy discussion is set that ignores that reality. The result is the frustration of policy discussion.

When I was visiting an authority, I was told by some of the officers that the councillors would never discuss policy. I met some of the councillors later — not around a committee table but informally. The talk touched on different topics, but they began to talk about cases they had been considering in their planning committee. The cases illustrated the conflict between conservation policy and their policy for economic development. In the discussion they in effect tested out the weight to be given to each of these policies.

They did not reach agreement on the right balance. They were not in agreement on what was acceptable. The did, however, agree on what was unacceptable. As they talked I realised that although they were discussing planning cases, they were discussing planning policies.

Before I left it was again said that the councillors never discussed policy. Perhaps the real problem was that they were not listened to when they did.

I have reflected on that discussion. There is a natural rhythm to policy discussion in local government involving political aspiration and management realities. The real art is to recognise that rhythm, not to constrain it to fit a model of how policy is to be discussed.

Yet the example is not isolated.

There are many authorities in which the folklore is that it is impossible to have a discussion of policy. Time and again it is said of councillors:

'We have tried to get them to discuss policy, but they are not interested.'

'All they are interested in is particular cases.'

Such are the complaints made as policy issues are dealt with on a long agenda in the formalities of the committee room, and the committee moves quickly from one item to another. Nor can it be said that the complaint is only made about councillors. Many a management team goes the same way:

'All we ever seem to discuss is the trivia.'

'The big issues are neglected.'

The difficulty of policy discussion may seem a strange complaint to some authorities. For in these authorities there is no lack of policy discussion — rather the reverse. The folklore there, is that there is plenty of policy discussion; there is almost nothing else. What is lacking is action.

Within those extremes there is a variety of experience. Not all that experience is as frustrating as these two extremes. Patiently and with difficulty, authorities have found ways of discussing policy in ways that relate to practice. That successful experience is easily dismissed:

'It may work there, but it wouldn't work here.'

'It wouldn't work with our councillors and our officers.'

It is important therefore, rather than holding out experience that will be rejected, to start with the reality of the problem.

The emphasis in this chapter is on the problem of lack of policy discussion rather than on the opposite problem. But from the analysis of this problem wider lessons can be drawn.

The setting for policy discussion

The setting must be appropriate to the role. The committee setting is appropriate for its own particular role. The committee is built for authoritative decision-making on action to be taken or recommendations to be made. The working of the local authority requires a focus for authoritative decision-making. But the setting appropriate for authoritative decision-making is not necessarily appropriate for policy discussion.

Authoritative decision-making requires its own formalities. The agenda, the reports, the committee room itself — all express that formality. Such a setting hardly assists policy discussion. Councillors and officers are imprisoned in the agenda. A good chair gets from item one to item 20 with as little trouble as possible; and an idea is trouble. Wide-ranging policy discussion disturbs the even flow of the agenda. An officer said:

'I actually wanted to know what they thought about item 14, but they were on to item 15 before anybody had a chance to say anything.'

But the business is done. Decisions are made, the minutes recorded. Authority is given for the work of the council.

▽ If you want business done, then have a committee room, an agenda and a chair who judges success by the number of items disposed of.
▽ If you want a good policy discussion then think again.

A An authority needs settings for getting business done but it needs different settings for policy discussion. Policy discussion needs more space than can be provided on a committee agenda for:

▽ ideas to develop
▽ issues to be explored
▽ consequences to be worked out
▽ differences to be argued through
▽ bases of agreements to be developed.

That space cannot be found in a normal committee meeting. Nor does the public scrutiny of the committee necessarily assist the development of ideas. Public expression of a tentative idea commits beyond intention, so the idea remains unexpressed.

Policy discussion is likely to flourish in settings

▽ not subject to the immediate pressure of decision-making, where discussion can be separated from decision;
▽ which permit those taking part to leave their formal roles at least a little way behind; a councillor does not even have to take the chair;
▽ which are not subject to the strict formalities of council business; discussion needs a structure to guide, rather than an agenda to be followed;
▽ in which time is available for issues to be fully explored; where the aim is to secure an organisational pause.

Such settings have been found. Opportunities can be created. Opportunities can be seized. There are no rules. The same people who sit in a committee apparently enclosed in its formalities can with a different stimulus engage in discussions very different to those constrained by the limits of the agenda. Authorities have found a variety of settings:

▽ the weekend seminar for all councillors to discuss the 'state of the authority', identifying problems and issues facing the authority;
▽ the seminar for a committee to discuss a policy issue before proposals are formulated, so that when the report is placed before the committee it will have been written with a full appreciation of members' views;
▽ the more formal meeting with only one item on the agenda, for discussion rather than decision;
▽ the working group of councillors or of councillors and officers set up to review policy in a particular area of concern and to produce options or recommendations for decision by a committee;
▽ policy review sessions, in which a group of councillors reviews a range of policies to establish priorities and changes required.

In all these examples, and the many others like them, the common element has been freedom from at least some of the constraints of committee working. Many councils are finding new settings for policy discussion. The organisational monopoly of the committee has been broken. From that experience lessons can be drawn.

Pre-conditions for policy discussion

1   *Settings must be appropriate to the discussion*
Policy discussions are of many different forms and, with the forms settings can vary. A policy discussion can be concerned with:

▽   issue identification to show where more detailed exploration of policy is required;
▽   an examination of how a controlling political party's aims can be translated into practical policy;
▽   a review of existing policies to establish where policy change is required;
▽   a specific problem to work out policy options.

The setting should vary with the purpose of the discussion. A wide ranging seminar involving all councillors discussing problems and issues confronting the authority meets the need of issue identification. The discussion of a party's aims needs a more structured discussion as does a review of existing policies. A working group meeting over a period of time is appropriate for a detailed working out of policy options.

2   *Policy discussion must be grounded in political reality*
Policy is made through the political process and settings must be structured to give recognition to that reality. Where there is clear party control, it will be appropriate for much policy discussion, although not all, to take place on a party basis. An examination of how a controlling party's aims can be translated into practice should take place first in discussion between councillors of the controlling party and the officers in informal settings. Such discussion must encompass both the political reality of the aims and the reality of any problems of implementations. Discussion fails if aims are not accepted because of problems or problems are not seen because of aims.

3   *Policy discussion requires its own structure*
Policy discussion is freed from the constraints of the committee agenda. That does not mean that a policy discussion does not need to be structured. Rather structure should be related to the requirements of effective policy discussion:

▽   for the generation of ideas, a catalyst who stimulates may be more important than a chair who controls;
▽   it is important that timing allows discussion to develop but not that discussion should be without purpose or time limit;
▽   discussion can be over-determined by background material, but a lack of background can make much discussion pointless;
▽   discussion can be helped over the longer term if the rhythm of discussion is changed. A weekend seminar needs a range of different methods of discussion to sustain interests: presentations, group discussions, brain-storming, etc;
▽   a committee layout to a room will create a committee discussion. Layout is important: chairs in a circle tend towards informality, whereas a table suggests more formality.

4   *Unfamiliarity and frustration must be tolerated*
Old habits die hard. Officers and councillors used to committees do not find it

easy to adapt to new ways of working. Those in a meeting will look for a committee agenda. Issues for discussion become an agenda to work through. If unfamiliarity leads to failure, experiment should not be abandoned. It is important to learn from failure as well as from success; perseverance is required.

However, the more policy discussion flourishes when it is freed from the pressures of decision-making and the constraints of an agenda, the more it requires an effective committee into whose agendas the results of discussion can feed. The relationship between the settings for policy discussion and the committee system has to be worked out. Without that there can be a growth of working groups, panels, and seminars at the expense of clear points of decision. Discussion may be good, but without results in practice the only product will be frustration.

Achieving policy discussion

The rhythm of policy discussion

In some local authorities new settings have provided the opportunity for good policy discussion and it has been recognised and welcomed. In others, however, there has been disappointment with the nature of the policy discussion. Despite the fact that organisational time and space has been created for policy discussions it is said:

'Oh, there was some good discussion but they would not face up to the real issues.'

'They focused too much on particular cases.'

'They wouldn't face up to the choice. They tended to fudge it.'

The complaint here is not that there was not a policy discussion but that the policy discussion was not a 'proper' policy discussion. This is a different issue from the failure that comes from unfamiliarity with the setting or from simple inexperience. For that the answer is perseverance. Here what is at stake is the nature of policy discussion.

Implicit in these comments is a model of what a policy discussion should be. It is assumed that it should:

▽ focus on general statements rather than on particular cases and
▽ make clear choices between conflicting aims

The frustration arises because the way that policy in local government is actually discussed does not fit the model. However what may be wrong is not the discussion, but the model. What may be required is a model that recognises the way that councillors wish to discuss policy rather than one that denies the validity of such discussions.

Too often when discussion focuses on particular cases, rather than on a general statement of policy, it is regarded as a refusal to discuss policy. Policy discussion, according to the model of 'proper' policy discussion, should be conducted at the level of generality. Yet general policy statements rarely have meaning by themselves. Policy is given meaning in the particular. To discuss particular applications of the policy is to test the policy.

Relating the general and the particular

It is only too easy to dismiss councillors who wish to discuss particular cases as not willing to discuss policy. It may well be that the councillors are discussing policy in the way they know best. They are trying to see what the policy would mean in practice. It is in practice that the policy has to be tested and it is in practice that they will feel the consequences. If the policy leads to unacceptable results then the policy should be changed.

▽   A new planning policy towards conservation is made meaningful by examining what it would mean to specific development control applications.
▽   A policy for school re-organisation to deal with declining school rolls is made meaningful by examining what it would mean for specific schools.
▽   A policy change about grants made to individuals is made meaningful by specific examples of its application.

Failure to recognise that the general is tested by the particular can lead to policy papers being imperfectly presented. A policy paper written in general terms may be accepted by a committee without appreciation of its implications. One of the most common complaints made is:

'It was only a few months ago that the committee accepted the policy, now they are objecting to its application.'

That remark by an officer may be more a criticism of a policy paper which did not give examples of specific applications than of the councillors' apparent change of mind. It was only in experience that councillors learnt of and tested the actual nature of the policy. The original paper did not permit that learning and the policy discussion did not allow that testing.

Similar difficulty arises in the consideration by an authority of sets of objectives. Sometimes objectives are based on such broad statements as:

'To provide an opportunity for all residents of the Borough to live in satisfactory homes in pleasant surroundings at a price that families can afford' or

'To enrich the lives of the people by the optimum personal development of each individual in the community'.

Local authorities have found such statements by themselves virtually impossible to discuss. They are so general it is impossible to see their practical consequences. For the same reason such general statements have little impact on action. Objectives can only be properly discussed if the consequences can be seen and tested. Objectives can only have a practical impact if those consequences are clear. Without that relationship they become a ritual statement that can be agreed to, but not discussed. Discussion of objectives may be better achieved by focusing upon the purposes of specific activities than on general statements that cannot be clearly related to such activities.

Some authorities have tried to use objectives as a basis for priorities in policy planning or in budgetary decisions. In such cases councillors are asked to attach priorities to different objectives. The assumption is that activities related to those objectives will then be allocated more resources. In practice councillors who have taken part in such exercises may often resist the consequences when these are spent out for particular activities. Again the problem lies in the failure to relate priority (general) to consequence (specific).

General statements of policy have to be given meaning in their application and tested in discussion if acceptance by a committee or council is to be a real acceptance. Discussion of the particular application of a policy is only a retreat if discussion of the particular has no regard for the general policy. To discuss particular cases and only particular cases is not policy discussion. But to discuss particular cases and then to consider their implications for policy is the most practical way that people have found to discuss policy. Policy discussion will be the more effective if such a rhythm is encouraged.

Discussion will flow from consideration of the policy to issues such as : What would that policy mean in practice? What would it mean in a specific case? What is the response to that meaning? — and on to: What are the implications of these cases for the policy? Should it be approved, rejected or amended?

The rhythm of policy discussion flows from general to particular and back again to general.

Policy choice and balance

In policy discussion a balance has often to be sought between conflicting policies, aims and purposes.

If there was clear agreement on one single objective and any proposed action was clearly related to that single objective, there would be little need for policy discussion. Agreement or disagreement would be clear. A choice could easily be made. But the real world of policy and its making is not like that as every councillor and officer well knows.

The search for clear choices between different objectives is rarely appropriate in the real world of policy-making. In that world a balance has to be sought. That is not the evasion that the model of 'proper' policy making suggests. To seek balance is to recognise that the reality of policy choices is rarely clear. A policy has to be balanced between different values, interests and aims. A budget is an exercise in balancing different activities and differing aims and purposes.

Different aims and purposes do not easily fit with each other. An action that meets one set of aims or policy may conflict with another policy. For example:

▽   A rural local authority may be in favour of conservation policies to preserve the attractiveness of its area, but also seek economic development to counter unemployment. The problem is not to decide wholly in favour of either objective, but to determine how far they can be reconciled and, if they cannot, the balance between these policies.

▽   An urban local authority has decided to pursue a policy of devolving power to local neighbourhoods, but the same authority has clear political priorities that it wishes to see applied throughout its area. The problem is not to decide totally for or against the devolution of power, but to determine the balance.

▽   In the organisation of social services there is a commitment to generic social work, but also a recognition of the need for specialist social workers. The issue is not to choose between the generic and the specialist social worker, but the appropriate roles for each.

▽   A library service has a policy of maintaining its book stock and its opening hours, but faced with a budgetary cut, it has to make a choice between those policies. The choice need not be an absolute choice, but can be on the appropriate balance between these policies.

Policy choice is rarely simple. The problem is often not to approve or to disapprove. The problem is to find the right balance. Activities conflict; policies challenge each other; objectives are not easily reconciled. In social services, concern for the family will not always lead to the same results as concern for the child. Roads construction programmes to secure improved transportation may create environmental problems. A new housing project designed to attract higher-income groups to the inner city may not assist existing residents. Freedom of the individual has to be reconciled with community concerns throughout the working of the authority; it arises in every planning application or every building inspected.

The problems of policy and action in local government involve choice, but it is rarely a choice for or against a particular policy. It is about achieving the right balance within a policy or between different policies. Aims have to be reconciled, values weighed and interests balanced. To secure policy discussion, the range of choice has to be identified and the balance explored.

Finding policy balance

In policy discussion balance is explored in specific cases. The balance between conservation and economic development can be explored through examples of the acceptable and the unacceptable. The balance between the devolution of power and authority policy is sought through the examination of specific issues. The balance between the generic and the specialist requires focus on particular needs. The balance between opening hours and book-stock requires the examination of actual examples. Balance cannot be achieved in the abstract, but through exploration of the particular.

Policy discussion should not be over-structured by the simplicities of choice but should allow the possibilities of balance between conflicting aims and purposes. Policy balance is not a compromise but is inherent in the nature of local government. It is the reality with which councillors and officers work.

In seeking balance in policy discussion the unacceptable is often more easily found than the acceptable. When there is disagreement about the balance to be sought in policy, it will not always be easy to reach agreement on what is correct. It may be possible, however, to identify imbalance. Between committed advocates of economic development and committed advocates of conservation, there may appear to be little scope for agreement. But few are committed in absolute terms. It is rather a question of different weights being given. To most advocates there will be forms of economic development that are unacceptable. Most advocates will not seek conservation at any cost. The area of the unacceptable can be identified even where there is no agreement on the area of acceptability. As with conservation and economic development, so it may prove between balancing individual freedom and community concern. Few deny that there are limits to individual freedom or that there are limits to community concern.

As with these, so with many other examples. In the structuring of policy discussion and the search for balance, a search for the unacceptable may prove more rewarding than a search for the acceptable.

Avoiding the necessity of decisions

Policy discussion need not be structured by the necessities of making decisions. It can lead to agreement but need not necessarily do so. It may lead to an elimination of the unacceptable — not the same as agreement — but even that need not happen. Where no agreement is reached, there should not be a presumption of failure. Policy discussion should not be constrained by the assumptions of decision-making.

Decision-making has its own structures, and those structures do not necessarily assume agreement. Decisions are reached through political processes of bargaining as well as being the result of discussion. Policy discussion does not remove the need for bargaining, nor will policy discussion be free from bargaining. And in the final resort the vote provides the means of decision, even where disagreement remains.

Yet the elimination of the requirements of decision-making lessens the immediacies of bargaining. There is no necessity for a decision. That lies elsewhere. The success of policy discussion lies in the issues explored rather than conclusion reached. That discussion will, however, inform the conclusion. The politics of bargaining will reflect the discussion.

The structuring of policy discussions should permit conclusion, but should not enforce it.

Guidelines for policy discussion

Discussion will not normally flow easily about a committee agenda. If you want business done, then have a committee meeting. If you want a good policy discussion, then leave the committee meeting as far behind as possible and remember the following:

B

∇ 1   The setting for a policy discussion should differ from the normal committee setting.

∇ 2   The rhythm of policy discussion is to move from the general to the particular and then back to the general.
— if they want to discuss the detailed implications of the policy, they are still discussing policy
— but one has to return to the policy, if the lesson is to be learnt.

∇ 3   It is easier to agree the unacceptable than what is acceptable, but that may be enough to start with.
— if they can identify what is unacceptable, they have identified the need for change
— the right policy will probably never be found; it may be enough to look for it.

∇ 4   Choice need not always be forced between conflicting policies, rather one can seek a balance between them.
— if choice is forced, it will not be carried into practice
— for balance is not a compromise, but a necessity.

∇ 5   There is a structure for discussion that differs from the structure for decision.
— discussion need not be structured for conclusion
— it should rather be structured for search.

∇ 6   If others think they are discussing policy, they may be right.
— if you think you know how policy should be discussed you may not be able to hear when policy is actually discussed
— the way that policy is discussed may be the only way the policy can be discussed; the secret is to work with the flow of discussion, not against it.

Conclusion

Local authorities are *political* institutions. Policy discussion expresses the political process but must be expressed in management action. Local authorities as *government* cannot pursue a single value, but have to balance values in political judgment. Local authorities as *local* government are close to the consequences of policy in the particular decisions. Policy discussion must be grounded in those realities.

Using this chapter

This chapter focuses on the nature of policy discussion in local government. It is meant to give understanding of how policy has to be discussed in local government. Those using the chapter should carry out the following exercises.

1   The setting of a policy discussion influences its nature. This can be illustrated by a committee meeting. Use or seek an opportunity to attend a committee.

How does the layout of the room, the procedures and the structure of the agenda influence the nature of the discussion?

Do you agree with the conclusions at A on page 102.

2   Policy discussions have a rhythm that has to be understood if they are to be developed. The main arguments of the chapter are set out at B on page 108. You should reflect on these. Use relevant material or experience that is available to you to test out the ideas, such as:

▽   reports to committees on policy issues;
▽   work on preparing such reports;
▽   discussions about how a policy item should be presented to councillors.

What assumptions are made as to how policy is discussed?
Do those assumptions fit the guidelines?
Any opportunity to attend or take part in policy discussions should also be used. In the light of this experience consider these questions:
Do you agree with the guidelines?
Which do you think are most appropriate or least appropriate?
Why?

Conclusion

It has been a simple message. Management in local authorities can only be understood through the purposes it has to achieve, the conditions which it has to meet and the tasks it has to carry out, and those purposes, conditions and tasks reflect both government and service. Without that understanding management is ineffective for local government.

The issues extend far beyond those explored in this book. They are merely examples to give understanding. Those who have developed that understanding will see many other issues.

So the book ends with a series of unresolved issues to which the reader or the author may wish to turn.

If equity is the fourth E, along with economy, efficiency and effectiveness, what are the implications for management?

How can a political strategy be given expression in management action?

Has marketing a role in a service where need exceeds resources?

Do the present budgetary processes of local government assist or hinder political choice?

Can performance measures express the achievement of political purpose?

How should one establish that value has been achieved in a value-for-money exercise in local government?

Is the management of rationing necessarily a key task for local government?

How can professional judgment and political choice be reconciled?

Can a shared sense of organisational purpose be achieved when political control changes and changes again?

And there are many other issues. That is the management challenge of local government.

Bibliography

Audit Commission (1984) *Obtaining Better Value in Education: Aspect of Non-Teaching Costs in Schools.*

Audit Commission (1985) *Obtaining Better Value from Further Education.*

Audit Commission (1986) *Towards Better Management of Secondary Education.*

Baddeley, S. and Dawes, N. (1986) 'Service to the Customer', *Local Government Policy Making* (March).

Barbour, George P. J. R., Fletcher, Thomas W., and Sipel, George A. (1984) *Excellence in Local Government Management*, Washington: International City Management Association.

Bowser, L. (1986) 'A local plan for central Newham: A positive role for planners and public'. Paper presented to INLOGOV seminar.

Bradford, City of (1984) *The Changing Face of Bradford* (District Trends).

Braintree District Council (1987) *Public Service Orientation, the Action Plan.*

Chase, G. and Reveal, E. C. (1983) *How to Manage in the Public Sector*, Reading, Massachusetts: Addison-Wesley.

Clywd County Council (1984) *South East Clwyd: A programme for action.*

Croydon London Borough (1985) *Primary Education in Croydon.*

Deven County Council (1985) *Information, management and planning strategy.*

Glennester, Howard (1983) 'Client Group Budgeting, a Prerequisite for Efficient Care', *Public Money* (December).

Hammersmith and Fulham London Borough (1985) *Marketing Financial Services to the Customer.*

Harlow District Council (1986a) *Community Voice.*

Harlow District Council (1986b) *Youth Inquiry Report.*

Heiser, Brian (1985) 'Qualitative Research with Users', *Local Government Policy Making* (March 1985)

Inner London Education Authority (1984) *Improving Secondary Schools* (The Hargreaves Report).

Jones, G. (1985) 'Performance Review of the GLC — a Model for the eighties', *Local Government Studies* (July/August).

Local Government Training Board (1985) (with the Audit Commission and the Institute of Local Government Studies) *Good Management in Local Government.*

Local Government Training Board (1987a) (by S. Leach), *Management Innovation in Smaller Shire Districts.*

Local Government Training Board (1987b) *Getting Closer to the Public.*

Manchester City Council (1986) *Poverty in Manchester.*

National Council of Voluntary Organisations (1984) *Client Rights*, London: Bedford Square Press.

National Consumer Council (1986) *Measuring up, consumer assessment of local authority service.*

Newcastle City Council (1985) *Social Audit 1979–84*.

Normann, R. (1984) *Service Management*, Chichester: John Wiley.

Nott, S. (1982) 'Unemployment alleviation at Shotton', *Local Government Policy Making* (Summer 1982).

Oxford City Council (1986) *A City Health Strategy, Report to Health and Environmental Control Committee*.

Rallings, S. and Thrasher T. (1983) *The County Council Elections in England*, (Plymouth Polytechnic).

Rallings, C. and Thrasher T. *The 1986 Metropolitan Borough Council Election Results* (Plymouth Polytechnic).

Richmond London Borough (1985).

Smith, J. (1985) 'Clients, users, consumers and members', *Local Government Policy Making* (March).

Vereker, G. U. P. and Tanner, B. M. (1975) 'Performance Review — an Inter-Agency Approach', *Corporate Planning* (November).

Vickers (1972) *Freedom in a Rocking Boat*, Harmondsworth: Penguin.

Warwickshire County Council (1982) *Public Relations and Warwickshire County Council*.

Windsor and Maidenhead District Council (1986) *The Royal Borough Way Ahead*

The Widdicombe Committee of Inquiry into the Conduct of Local Authority Business (1986), Research Volume 1. *The Political Organisation of Local Authorities*.

The papers on which the chapters are mainly based are

Chapter 1 Is Management in Local Government a Special Case (LGTB 1985).

Chapter 2 The Politics of Local Government: Implications for Management Development (LGTB 1984).

Chapter 3 The Growing World of Public Protest: Implications for Management Development (1986).

Chapter 4 The Management of Influence Implications for Management Development (1986).

Chapter 5 Public Service Orientation: Developing the Approach (LGTB 1986).

Chapter 6 Public Service Orientation and the Citizen (LGTB 1987).

Chapter 7 Public Service Orientation: Issues and Dilemmas to be faced (LGTB 1986).

Chapter 8 The Role of the Chief Executive: Implications for Training and Development (LGTB and SOLACE 1987).

Chapter 9 In Search of the Management of Education (LGTB 1986).

Chapter 10 Discussing Policy; Ideas for Improving the Formulation of Policy (LGTB 1987).

Index